How Writing Shapes Thinking

D0470214

How Writing Shapes Thinking

A Study of Teaching and Learning

Judith A. Langer
State University of New York at Albany

Arthur N. Applebee
State University of New York at Albany

National Council of Teachers of English
1111 Kenyon Road, Urbana, Illinois 61801

Book Design: Tom Kovacs for TGK Design

NCTE Stock Number 21802

Library of Congress Cataloging in Publication Data
Langer, Judith A.
   How writing shapes thinking.

   (NCTE research report; no. 22)
   Bibliography: p.
   1. English language—Composition and exercises—Study and teaching—Research. 2. English language—Rhetoric—Study and teaching—Research. I. Applebee, Arthur N.
II. Title. III. Series.
PE1011.N295 no. 22 [PE1404] 428'.007 s   87-24798
ISBN 0-8141-2180-2   [808'.042'0712]

Contents

List of Tables

Acknowledgments

Projects of this size are never easy. And they never go exactly as planned. What makes us undertake them time and again, though, is the special intellectual community that forms and pushes our thinking beyond what we could ever do alone.

We would like to thank the teachers who worked with us in the various parts of the project. Their dedicated professionalism and willingness to accept the risks of trying new approaches made the project possible. They have our deepest respect and admiration. To protect their privacy, we have not used their real names in the report that follows.

We were also lucky to have a team of bright, hard working, and eminently sensitive research colleagues who understand teachers, students, and teaching and learning theory well enough to have influenced our thinking, expressed on the pages you are about to read. We owe a debt of thanks to Russel Durst, Brian Gong, James Marshall, Kay Butler-Nalin, Deborah Swanson-Owens, John Shefelbine, William Sweigart, and David White, who were centrally involved in the planning, preparation, data collection, scoring, analyzing, conceptualizing, and synthesizing of initial results. Although starting after the data had been gathered, Arthur Hall, Rebecca Hawthorne, Tamara Lucas, and Paul Otteson were especially helpful in scoring, coding, analyzing, and reacting to our growing interpretations of the data. We thank them too. The thinking of all twelve is represented in these pages.

This project was funded by the National Institute of Education (presently the Office of Educational Research and Improvement), Department of Education. To them we owe the scholar's debt; but for them, this work would never have been. It is only with their support that work of this magnitude can be carried out. The opinions expressed herein do not necessarily reflect the policy or position of the National Institute of Education, and no official endorsement should be inferred.

Because this was a long-term project, some of the work has appeared in other forms, in other contexts. Published papers that we have drawn upon heavily include: Langer, Literacy instruction in American schools,

American Journal of Education (1984a); Langer, Learning through writing: Study skills in the content areas, *Journal of Reading* (1986a); Applebee, Writing and reasoning, *Review of Educational Research* (1984); Applebee, Problems in process approaches, National Society for the Study of Education, 85th Yearbook (1986); and Langer and Applebee, Reading and writing instruction: Toward a theory of teaching and learning (1986). These works are cited fully in the reference section. We have also written other papers about our ideas in progress. They are referred to when appropriate and cited in the references as well.

We have presented this work many times, to many audiences. In response, our colleagues have questioned us, pushed us to defend our statements, and in the end to reformulate our arguments. We thank them too. And we thank each other — each for putting up with the other through the trials and tribulations that a project of this magnitude entails.

I Overview

1 Introduction

In this study, writing assignments as part of the secondary school curriculum are examined to determine their use in fostering learning and integrating new information with previous knowledge and experience. Our previous studies have suggested that writing is rarely used in these ways, in part because as a profession we lack a clear understanding of the kinds of learning that writing can foster, and in part because we lack careful explanations of how to plan and carry out such activities. The present study seeks to address both those needs.

Our interest in the uses of writing in the school curriculum is based on our belief that the effective teaching of writing is an essential component in any successful school program: to improve the teaching of writing, particularly in the context of academic tasks, is also to improve the quality of thinking required of school children. In taking this view that good writing and careful thinking go hand in hand, we are hardly alone. Historians who have studied the development of literacy have cited the acquisition of writing within a culture as a fundamental factor in the development of modern thought — promoting in particular those types of discourse (and those types of thinking) we label "rational" or "scientific." They attribute this development to the fact that the act of writing facilitates a logical, linear presentation of ideas, and to the permanence of writing (as opposed to the fleeting nature of talk), permitting reflection upon and review of what has been written. Written language not only makes ideas more widely and easily available, it changes the development and shape of the ideas themselves. Following in this tradition, advocates of "writing across the curriculum" have stressed the role of writing in learning, and this approach is now gaining in popularity among both teachers and researchers (Applebee, 1977; Fulwiler and Young, 1982; Gere, 1985; Marland, 1977; Maimon, 1981; Martin, 1984; Martin, D'Arcy, Newton, and Parker, 1976; Newkirk and Atwell, 1982; Young and Fulwiler, 1986). Thinking skills are taught best when related to some content, the argument goes, and writing provides a particularly welcoming context for thinking deeply about such content.

3

Writing and Thinking

Growing acceptance of the role of writing in thinking, however, has not led to equal success in improving the teaching of writing or in developing reasoned and disciplined thinking among American school children. The most extensive data on student achievement in the United States come from the National Assessment of Educational Progress (NAEP, 1978, 1981; Applebee, Langer, and Mullis, 1985, 1986a, 1986b, 1987). Across a variety of assessments, the results suggest that American schools are doing a reasonable job of teaching lower-level skills; results from tasks requiring more complex reasoning skills, however, are much less encouraging. The 1981 report found that by age seventeen, most students were able to read a range of material appropriate for their age level and to formulate and express their initial interpretations of that material. Unfortunately, as the report stated,

> Students seem satisfied with their initial interpretations of what they have read and seem genuinely puzzled by requests to explain or defend their points of view. As a result, responses to assessment items requiring explanations of criteria, analysis of a text, or defense of a judgment or point of view were generally disappointing. Few students could provide more than superficial responses to such tasks, and even the "better" responses showed little evidence of well-developed problem-solving strategies or critical thinking skills. (2)

Our 1986b report on achievement makes it clear that the problem continues:

> A major conclusion to draw from this assessment is that students at all grade levels are deficient in higher order thinking skills. The findings indicate that students have difficulty performing adequately on analytic writing tasks, as well as on persuasive tasks that ask them to defend and support their opinions. Some of these problems may reflect a pervasive lack of instructional emphasis on developing higher order skills in all areas of the curriculum. Because writing and thinking are so deeply intertwined, appropriate writing assignments provide an ideal way to increase student experiences with such types of thinking. . . . Students need broad-based experiences in which reading and writing tasks are integrated with their work throughout the curriculum. (11)

Put simply, in the whole range of academic course work, American children do not write frequently enough, and the reading and writing tasks they are given do not require them to think deeply enough.

The role of writing in thinking can be conceptualized as resulting from some combination of (1) the permanence of the written word, allowing the writer to rethink and revise over an extended period; (2) the explicitness required in writing, if meaning is to remain constant beyond the context in which it was originally written; (3) the resources provided by the conventional forms of discourse for organizing and thinking through new relationships among ideas; and (4) the active nature of writing, providing a medium for exploring implications entailed within otherwise unexamined assumptions.

If this is correct, and if writing is so closely related to thinking, we might expect to be able to cite a variety of studies that support the contribution of writing to learning and instruction. Yet recent reviews of the relevant literature (see Applebee, 1984) make it obvious that there has been little research on this issue. Research on writing has been remarkably slow in examining the ways that writing about a topic fosters further learning about the topic. Two different traditions contribute to this lag in research: the first treats the process of writing as the rhetorical problem of relating a predetermined message to an audience that must be persuaded to accept the author's point of view. In this tradition the writing problem is one of audience analysis rather than of thoughtful examination of the topic itself. The second tradition assumes that the process of writing will in some inevitable way lead to a better understanding of the topic under consideration, though how this comes about tends to be treated superficially and anecdotally. Although we ourselves have enthusiastically advocated writing across the curriculum and related reforms, we have found no convincing research base for these programs.

Thus we began this study with two very broad types of questions. The first focused on the effects of different writing tasks on learning, and the second focused on classroom implementation of writing activities to support instructional goals in academic classrooms. The first set of questions asked: What contribution, if any, does written language make to intellectual development? Why, if at all, should we be concerned with the role of writing in our culture in general and in our schools in particular? To what extent should we strive to make clear and effective writing a "central objective of the school" (Boyer, 1983, p. 91)? If we do, can we assume that we will also be helping students develop the "higher order" intellectual skills and "skilled intelligence" demanded by the National Commission on Excellence (NCE, 1983)?

Writing and Instruction

Our concern with the role of writing in learning is part of our broader concern about the nature of effective instruction. Traditional approaches to the teaching of writing have been prescriptive and product centered, emphasizing the formal structure of effective discourse. At the sentence level, this approach has led to an emphasis on the rules of grammar and usage; at the text level, it has led to an emphasis on the characteristics of the traditional modes of discourse (narration, description, exposition, persuasion, and sometimes poetry). In its purest form, this approach consists of analyzing classic examples of good form, learning the rules that govern those classic examples, and practicing following the rules (either in exercises of limited scope or by imitating the classic models). In secondary school instruction, Warriner's *Handbook of English Grammar and Composition* (1951) is the archetypal example of this approach, and in its many editions it is the most widely used high school composition text today.

The 1970s and 1980s, however, brought a major change in accepted approaches to writing instruction. In direct opposition to the focus on the final written product, there was a groundswell of support for "process" approaches to the teaching of writing. Paralleling our general concern with writing as a way of thinking, advocates of these approaches emphasized the thinking strategies underlying the processes of composing a text. Still, the definitions of process approaches vary considerably from one teacher to another. In general, such approaches are marked by instructional sequences designed to help students think through and organize their ideas before writing and to rethink and revise their initial drafts. Activities typically associated with process approaches to writing instruction include brainstorming, journal writing, emphasizing students' ideas and experiences, small-group activities, teacher-student conferences, multiple drafts, postponing concern with editing skills until the final draft, and deferring or eliminating grades. For convenience in instruction, process activities in writing are often subdivided into stages such as prewriting, drafting, revising, and editing, usually with the caveat that the processes are recursive rather than linear, complex rather than simple.

Arising as a radical response to an overemphasis on the final written product, process approaches in their various manifestations have become the conventional wisdom, at least among leaders in the teaching of English. The journal literature of the 1980s has been dominated by suggestions on how such approaches can best be implemented, and influential programs such as the National Writing Project have helped to make such approaches more widely known.

Process-oriented approaches to writing would seem to have a natural affinity with our concern for the role of writing in academic learning. Both emphasize the active role of the writer, who must organize and reformulate ideas and experiences in the process of writing about them. Both treat learning as ongoing and cumulative, with errors to be expected (and even encouraged as a natural concomitant of tackling new and more difficult problems). And both imply renewed attention to the processes rather than simply the outcomes of instruction.

However, process-oriented approaches to writing instruction have not been widely adopted outside the English classroom (and even in English, they are more likely to occur in composition lessons than as part of the teaching of literature). As our previous studies have indicated, teachers of other subjects have few models of how such approaches to writing might work to foster academic learning in their classes. And teachers are understandably reluctant to devote much time to these approaches if they do not promote learning of the teachers' own subjects (Applebee, 1981; Applebee, Langer, et al., 1984). Teachers do not know what trade-offs would be required in their own instructional goals, or what benefits might ensue in terms of students' subject-area learning if they were to engage in more process-oriented writing instruction. At the same time, inquiry-based learning has been widely advocated in such subjects as science, social studies, and mathematics. There is a natural affinity between such emphases and the goals of process-oriented writing tasks, although the links between inquiry or process approaches in the subject areas and process approaches to writing instruction have not been carefully developed.

Further, recent reports have also indicated that process-oriented approaches to writing instruction have been relatively ineffective in helping students to think and write more clearly. Although some of the writing activities that students engage in have changed, these changes have not led to proportionate changes in achievement. Our report on the National Assessment results summarized the problem:

> Some students did report extensive exposure to process-oriented writing activities, yet the achievement of these students was not consistently higher or lower than the achievement of those who did not receive such instruction.
>
> Since students who plan, revise, and edit are more likely to be better writers, the NAEP results support the national emphasis on teaching the writing process. Students who use the kinds of process strategies we think teachers should be teaching have higher writing achievement. The results, however, do not indicate that classroom instruction in the writing process has been effective. This suggests that the new instructional approaches are treating the writing processes in a superficial manner. Students are not learning to link process activities with problems they face in their own writing. (Applebee et al., 1986b, pp. 12–13)

Thus the second cluster of issues that shaped the present study had to do with the implementation of process-oriented writing as part of subject-area teaching. Could such approaches to writing contribute to students' learning of new material in a variety of subject areas? What problems would teachers find in adapting such approaches to their own purposes? Are there common strategies that might be effective across a range of different teaching contexts? Or will each subject (or each teacher) have its own configuration of most useful writing activities?

The Research Agenda

To answer these questions, we took a two-pronged approach. One prong of our research examined the specific thinking and learning processes involved in various writing tasks, to learn whether writing in fact supports learning and, if so, to seek evidence of the different contributions that various types of writing activities can make to subject-area learning. Such research is essential before we can knowledgeably suggest that asking students to write is an important part of the teaching of subject-area content, not just a favor to the English department.

The other prong of our research examined writing and learning in collaborative classroom settings, with teachers working closely with the research team to find new ways in which extended writing could be integrated into their ongoing classroom activities. Originally, we conceived of this series of studies as analyses of the problems and benefits that subject-area teachers could expect in the course of broadening the uses of writing in their classrooms. We expected to emerge with a series of well-developed case studies that would provide models to which teachers could turn for help in the process of modifying their own approaches. But we were able to do this only in part. The teachers found that it was relatively easy to modify the pattern of activities in their classrooms, broadening the uses of writing in which their students engaged. But the teachers also found that in some cases such changes in classroom activities also led to a fundamental change in what counted as "knowing" a subject, and with that a reassessment of the role of the teacher and the role of the student in the whole pattern of classroom interaction.

Thus, rather than focusing solely on models of practice, this report has a broader theme: Recent reforms in the teaching of writing offer more than a series of new activities to achieve more effectively teachers' current instructional goals; they also have the potential to transform our conceptions of the nature of teaching and the nature of learning in school contexts. This is a larger agenda than we had bargained for; the discussions that follow are a beginning rather than a final solution to the questions we raise.

Overview of This Report

In the report that follows, chapter 2 provides a summary of the larger project, highlighting the data gathered and the kinds of analyses we undertook. Chapter 3 provides a detailed introduction to our observations of teachers and their students, with some general findings about ways in which they used writing in the teaching of academic content. Chapter 4 describes the types of writing activities that worked in a variety of content-area classrooms. (In so doing, this chapter comes closest to our original intention of developing models of successful teaching.) In chapter 5, our focus turns away from the activities provided and toward the redefinition of teaching and learning that occurred in the classrooms where writing worked best to foster academic learning. Chapters 6 through 8 examine the kinds of thinking and learning promoted by different types of writing. We describe the different ways that students deal with content based on the writing task they engage in and the different kinds of learnings that ensue. Chapter 9 brings together our concerns about the role of the teacher and the role of the learner in the instructional interaction, providing a theoretical framework, practical suggestions for an alternative model of instruction, and a discussion of the constraints that must be addressed if wide-scale use of writing to support learning is to become a reality.

2 The Project

NIE over 3 yrs

The project reported in this book was funded by the National Institute of Education and extended over a period of more than three years. It was motivated by our desire to better understand the role that writing plays in academic learning and also to identify particular ways that writing can be used more effectively in high school classrooms. Our work took two forms: we conducted a series of studies of teaching in which we studied a total of twenty-three teachers and their students as they used writing to foster learning in their academic courses, and we conducted a series of studies of learning in which we examined the effects of different kinds of writing tasks on academic learning.

Studies of Teaching and Studies of Learning

We began our studies of teaching with a survey of eighteen science and social studies teachers who were recommended because they had already incorporated writing into their classrooms; we wanted to learn more about the types of writing activities they used in their classrooms and the extent to which these activities aided students' learning about the particular subject at hand. We followed this survey with a series of in-depth studies of particular classrooms in action. In these in-depth studies, we collaborated with highly experienced teachers who wanted to incorporate additional writing into their instruction as a way to support academic learning. We saw these classroom studies as a process of collaboration to which we brought our knowledge of writing tasks and process-oriented writing instruction and to which the teachers brought their knowledge of their specific subject areas, as well as their understanding of the needs and interests of their particular students.

In the course of these studies, we lived as observers in eight secondary school classrooms (science, social studies, English, home economics) several days a week for periods ranging from five months to two years. Each individual classroom became a case study, documenting the effects of introducing new writing tasks specifically to further student understanding of new concepts as part of the regular

11

curriculum. We examined instructional planning, classroom activities, and curriculum coverage, as well as students' approaches to the new tasks. From each classroom we also selected individual students as case-study informants who reported to us their interpretations of the lessons, the ways in which they approached their work, and their understandings of the teachers' expectations as well as their own goals. Field notes and observation schedules, teacher interviews, student interviews, and writing samples provided the data for our analyses.

To learn more about the ways that writing tasks interact with what students are learning, our studies of learning traced the effects of various kinds of writing tasks on student engagement and learning. These studies used think-aloud self-report techniques in conjunction with more traditional tests of learning and recall to examine how learning new content is influenced by relevant background knowledge and by the type of writing task. In some cases, we studied individual students as they completed their regular classroom assignments. In other cases, we conducted experimental studies in which larger numbers of students engaged in writing and studying tasks that paralleled some of those being developed by the teachers.

Although we initially expected to carry out a series of studies that would address our original questions one by one, we found that the problems we were studying were too complex to permit this. Instead, each new analysis pushed us to ask questions we had not originally intended — and our treatment of the studies presented in this volume is a reflection of that. Rather than a simple report of findings, our discussion here is also a report of an evolving intellectual history.

The Teachers

Twenty-three teachers participated in this project. Of the eighteen involved in the initial survey, we selected two for the first year of classroom studies, one of whom continued to work with us in the second year. Five others joined us for the second year of classroom work. All twenty-three had been teaching for at least eight years; one had thirty-three years of classroom experience. While the initial eighteen had demonstrated their interest in writing through previous participation in Bay Area Writing Project workshops, the other five expressed similar motivations in volunteering to work with us. All wished to develop more effective ways of using writing to foster student learning of course content. The subjects they represented included English, science, social studies, and home economics.

The Students

In all, 566 students participated in the project. Of these, 326 participated in experimental studies of writing and learning, twenty were case-study students, and the remainder participated in the collaborating classrooms but not in the other parts of the study. They represented the typical range of student achievement levels generally found in working- and middle-class suburban communities in the San Francisco Bay area.

First-Year Activities

Studies of Teaching

Our work with the teachers began with an interview and observational study of the practices of eighteen Bay Area science and social studies teachers recommended to us for their unusual efforts to incorporate writing assignments into their curricula. This preliminary study served two purposes: it provided a baseline of data about the kind of writing taking place in the classrooms of teachers who had already begun to use writing in the content areas (reported in chapter 3), and it helped us identify one science and one social studies teacher to work more intensively with us during the first year.

As part of the project, these teachers developed writing activities that reflected their own curriculum goals and that were designed to support student thinking and learning about the course content. We worked with the teachers as they planned the activities, and we observed each class several times a week to learn how those activities were carried out — how the teachers presented them and how the students approached them. We gathered data from the teachers and students through baseline interviews, planning sessions, classroom observations, interviews with students, photocopying student work, teachers' logs, and end-of-year wrap-up sessions.

These activities were planned as a school-university collaboration in which the various participants contributed their particular expertise to the ongoing work. All of the participants agreed at the outset to explore a variety of ways that writing might be used to support academic learning — developing new activities and examining their effects on ongoing instruction and on student learning. To the collaboration, the teachers brought their knowledge of their particular subject areas, their ideas about how writing might be used in their classes, and their knowledge of their particular students and classrooms. The university-based project team added suggestions for structuring writing activities, as well as expertise in methods for studying classroom learning.

Activities were developed through collaborative planning sessions that focused on each teacher's goals and objectives in upcoming lessons. Usually, these sessions formulated a general approach to a new activity, which was then elaborated and implemented by the individual teachers in ways that they found comfortable and effective. After each activity had been introduced, discussions focused on understanding what had worked in terms of the teacher's goals, what had not worked, and why.

Studies of Learning

During the first year, we also conducted two studies examining student learning from particular writing tasks. The first was a pilot study, focusing on six students, to develop materials, procedures, and methods for analyzing student approaches to learning through writing. We wished to be able to describe how engaging in different writing tasks affects the organization of information, both in writing and in remembering. Specifically, we examined how the students' knowledge of a textbook passage was affected by the type of writing they engaged in after reading the passage, and the kinds of knowledge students called upon and the strategies they used in the act of making meaning through particular writing tasks. This study is described in chapter 6.

The second study gathered a larger sample of data about the effects that writing has on learning social studies. Because teachers (and instructional materials) often ask students to write in conjunction with their textbook reading, we were particularly interested in the kinds of learning engendered by the different writing activities that can be assigned after readings of textbook passages. We studied the effects that the various writing tasks have both on recall of specific information and on more general understanding (the ability to apply important concepts). Results from this study are reported in chapter 7.

Second-Year Activities

The procedures for data gathering and analysis developed during the first year provided a model for the second year.

Studies of Teaching

During the second year, we broadened our studies of teaching to include more teachers and more subject areas. At the suggestion of the teachers who collaborated with us during the first year, we concentrated in the second year on one school site. One teacher from the first year continued on, together with five of her colleagues who shared a common interest in developing writing activities that might foster learning of their subjects. They taught ninth-grade through twelfth-grade science, social studies, English, and home economics. Data collection followed the plan developed in the first year. Results from these studies of teaching are reported in chapters 3 through 5.

Studies of Learning

We also collected two further sets of data on student learning during the second year. Because we were interested in collecting data more fully rooted in ongoing class activities, one set of data consisted of think-aloud protocols gathered in the case-study classrooms. These protocols provided us with evidence of the kinds of thinking and reasoning the students engaged in when completing their classroom assignments. When the other students were engaged in writing activities in their classrooms, think-aloud informants left the room to tape-record their thoughts while completing the same assignments. Results from these analyses are included in chapter 4.

A second set of data was based on common writing-to-study-and-learn tasks we had observed being used in the participating classrooms. The intent in this study was to obtain objective evidence of the effects on student learning of writing-to-study tasks similar to those used regularly by the participating teachers. Content was introduced through textbook passages, followed by instructions to complete one of several study tasks. Our analyses focused on the interactions among the type of task, the specific content focused on, and later recall of the material. Results for this study are reported in chapter 8.

The Third Year and Beyond

Because of the size of the data set and the broadening focus of our concerns, additional analyses and reconceptualization were necessary when interpreting the results. This digestion, contemplation, and rethinking took place during a third and part of a fourth year. Earlier reports reflecting our developing perceptions have been published elsewhere (Applebee, 1984, 1986; Langer, 1984a, 1986a; Langer and Applebee, 1986), and are drawn upon here as needed.

The next chapter explains in more detail the methods we adopted in our studies of teaching, including the findings from our initial survey of eighteen teachers and profiles of the seven teachers who were our primary collaborators during the remainder of the project.

II Studies of Teaching

3 The Participating Teachers

Our studies of the teaching of writing began simply enough. They were an attempt to develop a series of detailed case studies that would serve as models for successfully implementing a broader range of writing-to-learn activities in subject-area classrooms. Our own past studies had shown that the major use of writing in secondary school classrooms is to evaluate students' learning (Applebee, 1981; Langer, 1984a). While this traditional role serves a worthwhile purpose, we wished to balance it with another, equally important use of writing — writing to support students' academic learning. As we will demonstrate in later chapters (6, 7, and 8), writing activities can provide varied and effective ways for students to think about and reformulate new learning and to integrate new information with their previous knowledge and experience.

Survey of the Uses of Writing among Content-Area Teachers

We began our project by examining how writing was used at its best — in the classrooms of science and social studies teachers who were interested in using writing in their classrooms and who had voluntarily and successfully participated in workshops that emphasized a wide range of writing activities. Eighteen teachers were recommended by teacher educators and district administrators for successfully integrating writing into their teaching. Of the eighteen, eight were science teachers and ten were social studies teachers; their teaching experience ranged from eight to thirty-three years. Three of the science teachers and seven of the social studies teachers had earned master's degrees, and all taught junior or senior high school in the San Francisco Bay area.

Procedures

Each teacher was interviewed for about three-quarters of an hour and observed for one class period. The interview covered several general areas: teacher background, changes in uses of writing activities since beginning to teach, difficulties in using writing activities, and resources available. In addition, the interview explored at some length the writing activity that each teacher reported using most frequently. Interviewers began by asking general questions and then used probes to investigate issues not discussed by the teachers. All interviews were tape-recorded. Whenever possible, observations were scheduled for days when teachers were working with the type of writing activity that they considered most typical of their teaching. Four research assistants conducted the interviews and observations.

Changes in Earlier Patterns of Teaching

We began our interviews by exploring how the teachers were currently using writing in contrast to how they had used it earlier in their teaching careers. The teachers who reported change seemed to have adopted activities presented to them as part of their inservice training. Fifty-five percent of the teachers reported that they were using writing more frequently. Some 50 percent also reported that they had changed their instructional approaches to include "process" activities such as prewriting, multiple drafts (often with teacher and student response to early drafts), using student writing as a model of good or expected writing, and using more class time for writing tasks.

Twenty-eight percent of the teachers mentioned changes in evaluating student writing, with several noting that they now commented on students' drafts without grading them. Comments on evaluation varied widely, however, and one teacher emphasized that evaluating for her had now become a matter of carefully grading the form in addition to the content.

These changes parallel those found in other studies of writing-project teachers (for example, Freedman, Greenleaf, Sperling, and Parker, 1985), as well as the changes in emphasis reported by students in the NAEP studies of writing (Applebee et al., 1986a).

Patterns of Instruction

While the science and social studies teachers reported taking a variety of approaches to writing in their classrooms, patterns within and between the two disciplines were evident. Operating out of different traditions and within different constraints, teachers in the two areas diverged somewhat in their willingness to use writing as an instructional tool. Science teachers, for example, were less likely than social studies teachers to perceive writing activities as falling within their curricular province. They felt, in general, more tied to a specific curriculum and spoke of their responsibility to cover a given number of topics during a school year.

Social studies teachers, on the other hand, were more likely to consider "skills instruction" — including writing skills — an integral part of their teaching agenda. They were more likely to emphasize underlying "concepts" and to separate the teaching of those concepts from "dates and places." Both the science and the social studies teachers felt they had little time or inclination to include many writing activities in their classrooms.

When the teachers did use writing, the content often became a vehicle for teaching conceptual skills rather than facts to be mastered by students. For example, a unit on the Great Depression in the United States provided an occasion for the students to discuss and write about poverty, government influence, and economics in general. While information about the Depression was used — and, the teacher hoped, remembered — the primary objective was the practice of broader conceptual skills that could be transferred to other social studies tasks. Students were considered successful if they had not only learned a set amount of information about the Depression, but could argue or write convincingly about it. Such uses of writing were rare, however, even in this highly select sample of teachers.

A closer look at the responses of the eighteen teachers reveals more differences. The teachers were asked to describe in some detail the kind of writing task they most frequently assigned to their students. We categorized these tasks along two dimensions, reflecting audience (self or teacher) and purpose (reviewing content area material or reformulating and extending it).

Assignments placed in the "self" category, although required by the teacher, were not formally graded. The primary purpose of these assignments was to provide students with an opportunity to work through a body of material. Some of the assignments asked students to review or summarize material in their own words; other assignments prompted them to reformulate and extend the material by constructing an argument or applying the information to a slightly different set of circumstances. Often, the assignments called on students to bring their own personal experience to bear on a particular concept.

Assignments placed in the "teacher" category were completed primarily for purposes of evaluation. Many of the same types of writing were called for as in the "self" category, but the teachers were primarily concerned with assessing the quality of the students' review or reformulation and with assigning an appropriate grade. Figure 1 displays the results of this categorization.

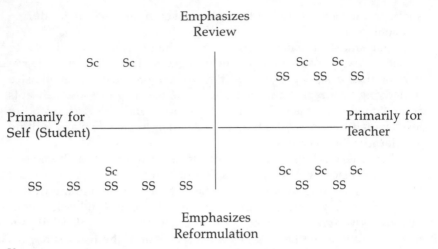

Figure 1. Writing tasks preferred by the science and social studies teachers surveyed.

In general, social studies teachers were more likely than science teachers to report assignments that asked students to write within a nonevaluative framework. Only one science teacher used such assignments to help students reformulate and extend material they were studying, and two others reported assignments that asked students to review material in their own words. More typically, five of the eight science teachers interviewed reported that their most frequent assignments were for evaluating students. In contrast, half of the social studies teachers reported that their most typical writing activities were nonevaluative assignments designed to help students extend and reformulate what they were learning.

Problems in Using Writing

Another section of the interview asked teachers what concerns, if any, they had about using writing in their classrooms. Two-thirds of the teachers worried about the extra time necessary for reading and responding to written material. Those who felt that all student writing should be read and corrected limited their use of writing accordingly. Others compromised, limiting their responses to general comments or simply reading less of what their students wrote.

Another group of teachers was concerned that students lacked sufficient writing skills to write extensively for their science or social studies classes. These teachers talked about students' poor language, grammar, and mechanics, as well as their lack of ability to write properly for the particular domains under study. This last concern was particularly widespread among the social studies teachers.

These findings prepared us for the kinds of complexity we would encounter in the next phase of our studies of teaching. Although there were some consistencies within subject areas, the teachers reported a wide array of uses of writing, and their interpretations of the uses and benefits of writing were often vastly different from one another's. In our past studies of the teaching of writing, we had focused on instruction in typical rather than exemplary classrooms. This survey made it clear that integrating writing assignments into academic classrooms was difficult, even for these exemplary teachers. Writing was used in somewhat limited and restricted ways and was often perceived as conflicting with the teachers' subject-specific goals. Constraints of curriculum and time were severe. We brought these concerns to our more intensive collaboration with individual teachers as we studied the kinds of writing that worked, as well as the factors that militated against writing in their classrooms.

Studies of Individual Classrooms

To examine the implementation of writing in content classes, we worked at length with individual teachers. During the first year, we worked with two, Jane Martin (social studies) and Julian Bardolini (biology), in different schools. Because these two teachers found it useful to talk to each other as well as to us, they suggested that during the second year we should concentrate on a single school, where such contact would be easier. This arrangement worked well for us, allowing us to study more teachers than we could otherwise have included. For the second year, we concentrated on Jane Martin's school, adding five new teachers: Kathryn Moss (chemistry), Janet Bush (biology), Bill Royer (social studies), Naomi Watson (home economics), and Jack Graves (English). We asked Jane Martin to continue working with us — as school coordinator as well as collaborating teacher.

The study was planned to investigate the ways that writing activities could further subject-area objectives. We wished to develop a clearer understanding of the kinds of learning that writing can foster in specific subject areas and also to develop a deeper understanding of how to carry out activities that could support these learnings. Members of the project team functioned as collaborators in the planning process: the

teachers brought their expertise in teaching and course content, and
the university-based staff brought their knowledge of the processes of
writing and learning. As a team, we studied how various types of
writing activities interacted with the dynamics of different classrooms.
The nature of the collaboration was based on the participants' differing
strengths: the teachers determined the content and objectives of their
courses, and the university-based staff suggested general approaches
that might foster the kinds of learning the teachers desired. Together,
we developed specific activities to work within individual classrooms.

We gathered case-study data to understand how the teachers'
objectives were translated into instructional plans, how these plans
were implemented in the teachers' classrooms, and how these activities
were then interpreted by the teachers and by their pupils. We used a
variety of methods:

Interviews were conducted with the teachers to learn about their
training and experience, their previous use of writing assignments,
their perceptions of the uses of writing in their classes, the construction
of their assignments, and the forms of evaluation each of them used.
In addition, we documented the nature and amount of writing taking
place in each classroom at the outset. Similar interviews were held at
the end of the project, further documenting the teachers' reactions to
the activities they had developed.

Case-study students were selected in each classroom to provide more
detailed information about students' reactions; equal numbers of more
successful and less successful students in each class were nominated
by the teachers. Weekly interviews were held with these students
throughout the study. They were interviewed about the amount and
kind of writing done in their other subject classes and their reactions
to the writing they were asked to do in the target class. Four students
participated in the case studies in each of the two classes during the
first year. With six classes to study in the second year, we reduced the
number of case-study students to two in each class. For selected
assignments, the case-study students engaged in think-aloud self-
report activities while their classmates were completing the same
assignments in their classrooms. This permitted us to study the cognitive
processes the students invoked and the knowledge sources they relied
on when engaged in the assigned activities. (Appendix 1 describes the
system we used to analyze these protocols.)

Planning meetings were held regularly, focusing on the goals for
upcoming lessons and on the ways that writing activities might be
used to further those goals. In these meetings, the university-based
team members served as a resource that the teachers could collaborate

with as they brainstormed new approaches and how to put them into practice.

Classroom observations were scheduled regularly in each classroom, focusing on lessons when writing activities were planned.

Writing samples were collected at regular intervals. These included all writing completed by the case-study students, as well as sample assignments from each class as a whole.

Wrap-up sessions were held at the end of each year, during which the participating teachers discussed the project with one another as well as with the project team.

Student writing was photocopied, interviews and meeting sessions were tape-recorded, and field notes were taken throughout our work with each classroom.

The Setting

We conducted the study in two suburban high schools, using ninth-grade through twelfth-grade students in science, social studies, home economics, and English classes. Although both schools had a heterogeneous student body, Julian Bardolini's school was the more affluent and higher achieving of the two. Most of the school's approximately 1,700 students graduate from high school and about 85 percent go on to college. It has a relatively low minority population, about 5 percent.

Jane Martin's school served about 2,100 students. It was composed of 25 percent minority (primarily Hispanic, South Pacific, and black) and 75 percent white students. Generally 90 percent of those students entering their senior year graduate, and 50 to 60 percent of the graduates go on to college. When our project began, this school had just absorbed the teaching staff and student body of a nearby high school that had been closed the previous year. Four of the six project teachers at this school were part of this shift: Martin participated in the project during her first and second years at the new school, and Kathryn Moss, Janet Bush, and Naomi Watson joined the project during their second year at this school.

Four criteria guided our selection of the collaborating teachers: they (1) were experienced teachers highly respected by their colleagues; (2) showed sympathy with and interest in the project's goals; (3) expressed a willingness to experiment with new approaches; and (4) taught in departments, schools, and districts that provided a supportive environment for change. The teachers received modest honoraria for their participation on the project team.

criteria for choosing tchers

Procedures

During the first year, initial meetings with the teachers began in January, and the project continued until the end of the school year. During the second year, initial meetings were held in November, and the project continued until April (the end of the third marking period). After agreeing to participate, each teacher selected one class to be the focus of our work.

To provide multiple perspectives, each university-based staff member worked in two classrooms, and each classroom had two university-based staff members regularly assigned to it. Although responsibilities were divided between studying the teacher and studying the case-study students in each class, the second staff member provided an ongoing backup in the case of scheduling problems or illness — as well as a helpful additional perspective when our understandings of each classroom began to emerge.

The collaborative nature of the project required the development of close working relationships between the participating teachers and the university-based staff. In the formal structure of the project, the primary collaboration took place during regularly scheduled planning sessions. These sessions centered on the teacher's plans for the coming days and weeks: the content that needed to be covered, the teacher's objectives for student learning, and the activities and materials that the teacher would generally use. Together, the teacher and the university-based staff would discuss ways that writing activities might be used to further the teacher's objectives for the unit, including discussion of how well previously introduced activities had functioned and how such activities might be recast to make them work better. Suggestions could come from anyone in the group; there was no "project" curriculum or set of "project" activities that the teachers were being asked to use. Instead, each planning team drew on the previous knowledge and experience of all of the team members to shape activities that seemed to make sense. The teacher would take the ideas that emerged from the planning sessions and draw on them as he or she developed specific daily lessons — modifying them as needed in the light of further reflection or the progress of the class for which they were intended. Usually, the planning sessions involved a single teacher and one or both of the university-based staff working in the same classroom. When problems developed, however, or if ideas seemed to be running short, other teachers and university-based staff were asked for new ideas.

Contacts between the participating teachers and the university-based staff quickly expanded beyond the formally scheduled sessions

Table 1

Types of Data Related to Students' Assignments

Source of Data	Focus of Analysis
Planning sessions (field notes, recordings)	Project goals Instructional goals
Observation of related lessons (field notes, teacher's log)	Implementation of goals Social context of classroom
Student interviews (field notes, recordings)	Student perception of activity Problems, approaches
Think-alouds (recordings)	Approaches to writing
Drafts, final products (photocopies)	Audience, purpose, content, quality

to include informal discussions in the staff room, at lunch, and on the telephone to review recent activities and plans for the next day. One of the teachers captured the spirit of these conversations when she commented at the end of the project: "We used the class as a laboratory. That was the way I saw it. It was wonderful to have people at my level as teachers to work with — having two other people's points of view."

The classroom observations, interviews with students and teachers, and writing samples yielded information about many different aspects of the classrooms and assignments we were studying. The various data sets and the focus of our analysis of them are summarized in table 1.

During the two years of this study, data were collected and analyzed from 89 planning sessions, 162 classroom observations, 160 student interviews, 47 think-aloud protocols, and 1,131 writing samples. The data collected from each teacher, as well as the general characteristics of each classroom, are summarized in table 2.

Analysis of Data

The study generated large quantities of information about the teachers and their classrooms. We organized these various sets of information around tasks-within-teachers. In other words, the various data sets were keyed to the individual task or assignment, providing multiple views of each task and allowing us to show the evolution of tasks from many perspectives for each teacher over time. These perspectives are illustrated in figure 2.

Table 2

Summary of Data: Case-Study Teachers

Teacher	Subject	Grade	Student Ability	n	n	Classroom Observations, Months	Planning Sessions	Student Interviews General	Protocol	Writing Samples
Year One										
Bardolini	Biology	10-11	Average	28	32	5	14	64	0	180
Martin	World culture	9	Mixed	33	28	6	12	55	0	220
Year Two										
Martin	World culture	9	Mixed	30	15	5	10	6	8	139
Royer	U.S. history	11	Mixed	36	15	5	8	6	9	139
Graves	English	9	Honors	16	18	5	9	8	11	84
Watson	Survival skills	12	Lower	30	18	5	6	9	10	191
Bush	Biology	10-12	Average	33	16	5	15	6	6	138
Moss	Chemistry	10-12	Average	22	20	5	15	6	3	40

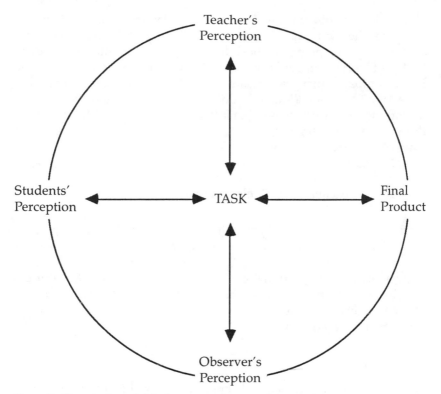

Figure 2. Organization of data from several perspectives.

With two university-based staff members and one teacher in each classroom (and with each staff member studying two different classrooms), we also had various perspectives on each classroom. For the qualitative data, analysis followed a systematic pattern of weekly write-ups of observations, synthesis of what had been observed, tentative interpretations, and a continuing testing of those interpretations through further observation. Initial syntheses were organized on the level of the individual teacher; final analyses involved identifying cross-classroom patterns of ways that particular types of writing assignments were used, revised, or rejected. At this point the qualitative analyses were also coordinated with the quantitative data from analyses of writing assignments and student think-aloud protocols.

The classroom data provided pictures not only of the classrooms as systematic and logical places of learning, but also of the central concerns that governed each teacher's decisions. Initial write-ups of our work with each teacher were prepared by the university-based project staff members most directly involved in each classroom: James Marshall prepared the write-ups for Jane Martin and Bill Royer; Deborah Swanson-Owens prepared those for Naomi Watson and Jack Graves; William Sweigart prepared those for Julian Bardolini, Janet Bush, and Kathryn Moss. Other staff members working in the same classrooms were John Shefelbine (Julian Bardolini), William Sweigart (Jane Martin during the first year), Russel Durst (Jane Martin and Bill Royer during the second year), Brian Gong (Janet Bush and Kathryn Moss), and David White (Naomi Watson and Jack Graves).

The Seven Teachers and Their Central Concerns

During our collaboration with the seven teachers, we gained an increasing understanding of them as experts in their subject areas, as educators with their own views of teaching and learning, and as individuals operating within the institutional constraints of their schools and districts. The brief sketches that follow provide an initial indication of each teacher's unique qualities and concerns, as well as of the commonalities among them.

Jane Martin

Martin was an enthusiastic collaborator during the entire two years. She took a leadership role in the second year of the project, enlisting, supporting, and encouraging the five other teachers in her school.

She had earned a bachelor's degree in history and sociology and a master's degree in history. When she began working with us, she had twenty-three years of teaching experience in grades seven through twelve. For the previous sixteen years she had worked in the same district, and she planned to remain there. She was extremely well regarded by her district's faculty and administration as a master teacher and dedicated professional; in June of her first year in the project she was appointed chair of her fourteen-member social studies department.

Martin's strengths as a teacher were easy to observe. She had a dynamic classroom presence, with a strong command of her subject matter and a warm, almost familial, rapport with her students. Throughout her teaching experience, she had remained open to new teaching ideas, including those sponsored by this project; she used our presence in her classes as an occasion to reexamine strategies and habits long in place. During the two years of the project, we studied one of her ninth-grade world culture classes.

During the two years we spent in Martin's classes, we came to characterize the central concern governing her classroom decisions as a desire to protect her students from error. She saw her job as teaching her students the requisite social studies material — they needed to learn a body of knowledge that was prescribed by the social studies curriculum. However, her instructional activities, plans, and interactions revolved around ways to teach that knowledge *without letting any students fail at any task.* Her role as teacher was to impart knowledge, to structure discourse and experiences in an orderly way, and to assess the students' mastery of the knowledge imparted. To protect her students from failing, Martin structured each activity around segments requiring only information the students already had. She provided the content and structure; the students needed to select the right information to insert into the outlines and exercises provided.

This desire to provide enough structure to protect her students is reflected in an assignment she developed to go with an animated video of *Animal Farm* — an assignment that emerged as Martin began to move her writing assignments away from simple review of new material toward more complex writing tasks. While they were watching the film, she asked her students to jot down examples to support three assertions:

1. Communism is based on the belief that people working together will accomplish more than people working individually.
2. No revolution achieves all of the goals it hoped it would.
3. The names given the animals tell the viewer a lot about the author's biases.

After collecting the students' worksheets, Martin selected the assertion for which each seemed to have the best examples. The following day she used the board to structure the paper they were to write:

Formula Paper

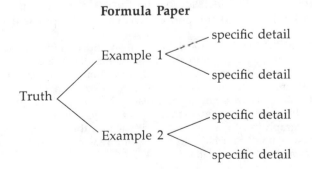

She explained, "Today you're going to write a really good two-paragraph paper for me. Instead of being free, it's going to be a formula. I'm going to tell you exactly where to put things." She then proceeded to do exactly that, demonstrating how the formula could be fleshed out by using the truth that "Good triumphs over evil" and examples drawn from the story of "Snow White." Fifteen minutes into the period, she turned from "Snow White" to the worksheets on *Animal Farm:*

> Now, I gave you three broad truths on your worksheet and I asked you to write examples that would prove any of those truths. I took those home and [next to one truth] I have written "go ahead," which means you have given me two good solid examples and details. I want you to write two paragraphs, one about each of the examples, proving the truths.

During the remainder of the period, the students used the examples and details Martin had approved to complete their essays with the formulaic structure she had provided. The result was a set of reasonably coherent expository paragraphs from virtually everyone in the class.

Most of the discourse that took place in the class represented a cooperative enterprise: Martin supplied the purpose and the structure, and the students supplied the information necessary to fill in that frame. She believed that the students did not know enough about what they were studying to be asked to develop new concepts on their own. Her approach to teaching was to transmit academic knowledge to her students gradually through a structured approximation to the kinds of tasks she hoped they might someday be able to accomplish on their own.

During the project, Martin developed activities that would help her students explore concepts and materials in a written language of their own. The increased chance that students might sometimes fail at a task conflicted with some of the basic tenets of her classroom discourse. She struggled with this issue of structure and control throughout her two years with us. At the end of two years, she put it this way:

> I think assignments have to be open-ended. I think the more structure you build into the assignments, the more you control them, and I do too much of that. They should have less structure in them. . . . But there's a good reason for structure in the teaching of "how." There's not a good reason in the teaching of "what." In the teaching of how that's OK. A kid has to know that a paragraph has to lay out where it's taking the reader, and if you make a point you have to have some reasons — more than one reason — to support it.

Part of Martin's struggle, however, was learning to separate the "how" from the "what." It was also difficult for her to find a workable balance between providing enough support and taking too much control.

Julian Bardolini

Bardolini was a teacher of biology and life sciences. He held a bachelor's degree in biology and had been teaching for twenty-two years. For the last fourteen years he had taught in his present school, where he was part of a twelve-member science department. During the year we worked with him, he taught two classes in advanced placement biology, two in general biology, and one in life sciences. The project focused on one of his general biology classes, which was made up of twenty-eight students.

During our year with him, it became clear that his central concern in planning his teaching was to provide his students with the basic factual information necessary to understand the biological sciences. He felt that his students had no knowledge of what they needed to learn and that the information itself was difficult for them to understand. Because Bardolini considered the assigned textbook too difficult, he relied on himself as the primary source of information; in each of the class sessions we observed, he used a lecture format, stressing the information he felt was most important for his students to learn. He thought some topics such as sexual reproduction were inherently more interesting to his students, and he spent more time on those topics than on others.

Before working with us, Bardolini had used a variety of writing activities, including essay tests, responses to chapter questions, lab reports, and required note-taking. His treatment of this work reflected his overall focus on basic factual information: "I just grade for the information — for the content of the material." He used the essay exam to test "for knowledge at the end of a unit; it's not normally just for writing something for the learning without getting evaluated on it." These essays were graded by teachers' aides who used correction guides that he had prepared as templates to check for correct words and phrases. His comments on work in progress pointed students toward content that needed to be added or, in the case of lab reports, tried to help them "understand the correct procedure."

Bardolini gave students points for everything they did in his classes. As he explained, "I don't think I have to evaluate all the things they do when they write. But students are so used to having things collected and graded, unless you give them a point on it they won't do it."

When the study began, his students were less than enthusiastic about written work in his classes. As one of the case-study students described it, "It's kind of a waste of time [to write in class], and it brings your grades down. No one can usually fit it together, what they want to say. They know what they're writing about, but can't write it down the way he [Bardolini] wants it to be written."

As Bardolini himself intended, the "way he wanted it to be" was the main source of authority in his classroom; when we questioned students about the source of their knowledge of biology, the teacher emerged as much more central than their books or their lab experiments.

During the project, Bardolini sought to broaden his repertoire to include writing activities that would engage the students in thinking about the material they were studying, as well as activities that would help them organize and remember the information he was presenting.

Kathryn Moss

Moss held a bachelor's degree in chemistry and two master's degrees, one in biochemistry and one in education. In twelve years of teaching high school, she had taught a range of science courses including chemistry, physics, biology, advanced biology, life science, general science, and physical science. She had written some of the syllabi for her district and had worked with the entire range of students. She was one of the teachers who had been transferred to her present school the year before we met her. The project focused on one of her chemistry classes.

When we met Moss, her classes were a mix of lecture, discussion, and lab work. Her view of her subject emphasized the process of inquiry, although she felt that this process was constrained by (and constrained to) the students' understanding of the formal body of knowledge of chemistry. Students worked in pairs in lab experiments, although each kept a separate lab book. She told us that she used writing more often when she taught biology than when she taught chemistry: "Part of my written and unwritten objectives for those biology classes is that [the students] become more literate in terms of specifically expressing ideas and in terms of analyzing articles they read." But in chemistry, she was unsure how to approach such goals — and was not convinced they were even relevant.

The primary difficulty, Moss felt, was that her students had no relevant knowledge about the subject upon which to draw. Chemistry was formally structured, and those structures had to be learned before the process of inquiry could become meaningful. Given the subject matter structure, the labs, and her perceptions of the students' lack of knowledge, writing seemed irrelevant to her purposes. The previous year she had tried using learning journals and had found them unsuccessful because the students did not focus on the critical issues, nor did they give her feedback to help her make constructive change in the curriculum:

> What I got back from them were strokes for me, which is what they thought the learning journal was supposed to be, and that's not what my idea was. I thought it was an exchange of ideas that was not only about their feelings regarding nuclear power and nuclear power plants and environmental issues, but . . . some dialogue about the constructive changes in the curriculum because I didn't particularly like the way the unit was done. I wanted some suggestions from them about how I could rearrange the unit a bit.

Moss had also tried research reports. They did not work either, because "It was the usual — to the library and copy down the encyclopedia — which offends me a great deal." After these negative experiences, she had never used these writing activities again. However, she did value the scientific approach in learning, wanted to foster student inquiry, and was curious to see if writing could help her do this. She was a willing if somewhat skeptical participant in the project.

Janet Bush

Bush held bachelor's and master's degrees in science with a minor in education. Early in her career, she had received a Ford Foundation fellowship and worked as a researcher for four years. Since beginning to teach, eight years before, she had taught life science, physical science, biology, advanced biochemistry, and physics at the high school level. She had taught the full range of ability levels. When she joined the project, she was beginning her second year in her new school; the project focused on her general biology class.

Like Kathryn Moss, Bush valued student inquiry but, unlike Moss, she felt she could begin this in the class she was teaching. She took her classes on field trips, emphasized lab and project work, and had experimented in the past with a variety of types of writing. In the initial interview, Bush said that essay exams used to be her primary form of extended writing in her classroom, but that she had stopped using them when her student enrollment exceeded thirty-five.

Even before we met her, she had used writing in many of her classes. She was enthusiastic about what writing could do in terms of her own subject-matter goals, and she had a number of ideas she was anxious to try out. Bush said she wanted to begin with "cognitive writing drills" before a lesson on an assigned topic to see what the students already knew, or after a lesson to help them think about what they had learned and then to reorganize it. She described what she meant:

> One other thing that I want to start doing . . . there are these things called cognitive writing drills, five-minute freewriting. The student has to take a pencil and write on the topic for five minutes without lifting the pencil. I want to incorporate that into some units, say start the unit with it — see what the kid already knows about the subject — and then see when they get done if they reread it and say "Oh, yeah that was right" or "That was wrong" or "I knew all this stuff already." Or to use it as part of the review of the unit, to see if they can write down everything they know and then go back and put it in a logical form and see if it helps them any. I'm curious about that.

Throughout the year, Bush was enthusiastic and creative about ways in which writing could extend her students' learning.

Bill Royer

Royer had earned a bachelor's degree in history and had done additional graduate work at several universities. He had taught social science for twenty-five years, with experience in grades nine through twelve. He had worked in his present school for seventeen years, combining his duties as a teacher and head football coach. Although he had taught a wide range of social studies courses in the past, for the last several years he had taught U.S. history and ninth-grade world culture. The project focused on his eleventh-grade U.S. history class.

In his initial interview, Royer indicated that his students generally did some writing each week. He used a textbook that took an inquiry approach, and his writing assignments required the students to pull together evidence from various sources and form opinions of their own. In all our discussions, he seemed aware of various instructional purposes that writing might serve, arguing that writing "requires the students to do some thinking" about issues in his course.

After twenty-five years in the classroom, Royer had fallen into a set of routines with which he was comfortable, which he saw as inquiry-based, and which he saw few good reasons to change. Finding time in his units for additional activities was difficult. Most of his units were very tightly planned, and completion of the planned activities played an important role in his judgment of whether he had had a successful school year. During the project, he worked to develop additional writing assignments that would strengthen rather than supplant the activities that he had already planned.

Naomi Watson

Watson had taught home economics courses for twenty-three years, moving to her present school during the first year of the study. She joined the project team the next year, when we studied her survival skills class. This course focused on the practical knowledge students need when they look for work and move away from home. Much class time was devoted to such enterprises as job hunting, banking, making consumer decisions, seeking legal council, and paying taxes.

> I try to gear the class to what I and my students think are some essential living skills, things the students really need to know — very practical things that will give them confidence in going out or looking for a place to live or choosing a roommate, and being able to communicate with somebody else.

Watson saw her professional life as her own means of survival: confronted with the picture of a newly widowed sister, she had decided twenty-three years before that she must always be prepared to take care of herself and so took courses in interior design and education in Oklahoma, Oregon, and Iowa. She hoped to teach her students the lesson she had learned twenty-three years before.

The central concern governing Watson's teaching was to help her students organize the material they were studying so that they could locate and retrieve it when needed. Absorbing information was of less importance: "I don't think everything has to be in your head. Of more value is knowing that you have a lot of different ways to tackle a problem." In her mind, knowing how to survive depended less on the facts one possessed than on the potential one had for accomplishing necessary tasks. She wanted her students to recognize "how and where to get information." With this as her goal, she concentrated on getting her students to organize their notebooks so that they would be valuable reference tools.

Watson's class was activity-based, using practical artifacts and activities wherever possible. She had been using a variety of writing activities in her classes well before we met her. She generally had a guest speaker once a week, and the students took notes on each presentation. They also wrote answers to study-sheet questions and sometimes wrote three- to five-sentence responses to homework questions. Some sort of writing occurred in class each day, and this writing became part of the students' growing reference notebooks. She collected these notebooks periodically to be sure that students were attempting the assignments.

Like Jane Martin, Watson took a personal interest in her students. She cared about them and their future — she worried about what they did not know and tried to provide structure to help them learn. However, unlike Martin, who was interested in helping her students acquire social studies concepts, Watson focused much more on organizational and interpersonal skills. For her, new knowledge develops from new experiences generated and monitored by the teacher. Like Martin, she felt it necessary to provide much of the content and to control much of the structure in classroom tasks, including writing.

During the project, Watson worked to develop writing tasks that would provide more opportunity for the students to present their own ideas — a shift in focus that she found difficult. At one point, for example, she discussed ways she might use writing in a unit on consumerism. She decided that the students would become more sensitive to the content being studied if they first did a freewriting on the topic. She spent thirty-three minutes on the freewriting, but devoted the major portion of the time to giving directions.

Jack Graves

When we met Graves, he had been teaching English for eighteen years. After graduating from Princeton with a bachelor's degree in literature, he had begun teaching in a special program for delinquent boys in Los Angeles. Later, he obtained teaching credentials from Stanford and began to teach at his present school, where he had taught a variety of remedial and advanced classes. The project focused on one of his freshman English classes.

Graves saw himself as primarily a teacher of literature, and his class was structured around traditional literary forms. He believed that there are correct interpretations of texts that need to be understood by the students in order to move them beyond "the mundane" and that it was his job to introduce his students to these traditional interpretations.

Writing in his class usually revolved around topics related to the texts being studied. These assignments were supplemented by writing about topics that drew on personal opinions or experiences, but these remained apart from the main agenda of the class. For their formal writing, the students worked on rough drafts in pairs that functioned as editing groups. The purpose of these groups was to "polish" the students' drafts — though Graves complained that he still found too

Table 3

The Teachers' Central Concerns

Teacher	Subject	Central Concerns
Martin	World culture	Protect students from error
Bardolini	Biology	Provide information
Moss	Chemistry	Foster content inquiry
Bush	Biology	Foster content inquiry
Royer	U.S. history	Complete established instructional routines
Watson	Survival skills	Help students organize
Graves	Freshman English	Develop understanding of traditional forms

many mistakes when he examined the work the students then handed in. Essays were given separate grades for mechanics and content, the latter focusing on the extent to which students understood accepted interpretations and followed the organizational guidelines that Graves provided as part of each assignment. One of his concerns was that his assignments were often "one-shots," with little connection from one to another. Thus one of his goals in the project was to develop sequences of activities that would help students develop ideas for their major papers.

Discussion

From the initial survey of eighteen teachers, we began to see two patterns emerging. First, there appeared to be differences between science and social studies classes both in the kinds of writing and in the ways that writing was used. Second, the uses of various kinds of writing tasks were teacher-specific: the tasks the teachers used and the ways they used them varied within as well as across disciplines.

The findings from the initial survey were reinforced by our case studies of individual teachers. As we can see in the brief portraits already presented, each of the teachers brought to the teaching day a somewhat different set of central concerns and a somewhat different conceptualization of his or her role as a teacher and the students' roles as learners; these differing views are summarized in table 3. How the teachers went about their teaching differed — and these differences were a sensible outgrowth of what they considered important for their students to learn.

For example, Martin and Royer were both social studies teachers, and both wanted their students to learn important social studies concepts through inquiry-based activities. However, Martin's central concern to protect her students from making errors and Royer's reliance on his previously planned activities led to instructional environments in which writing took on different meanings — what was assigned, how it was assigned, and how it was interpreted and evaluated were shaped by the central concerns of each teacher.

We can also see this in the science classrooms. All three science teachers (Bardolini, Moss, and Bush) wanted their students to learn the basic information of their sciences; they felt such knowledge provided the base for more independent inquiry. However, while Bardolini's desire to provide information precluded activities that required the students to go beyond those facts, both Moss and Bush considered such activities central to science learning.

Across classrooms, the most important determinants of the uses of writing were the teachers' underlying notions of teaching and learning. Our understanding of the teachers' central concerns provided important insights that helped us interpret the results of our studies of writing in their classrooms. Reports of these analyses are presented in chapters 4 and 5.

4 Writing in Academic Classrooms

We have seen in the previous chapter that the classrooms of the seven collaborating teachers were governed by somewhat different central concerns, ranging from leading students to understand the principles underlying inquiry in a scientific discipline to introducing them to the traditional organizing features of English language and literature. In studying the writing activities that could foster subject-area goals within these classrooms, we found that they were similarly varied. Simple activities like freewriting exercises or journal keeping were used in different ways by each teacher; more extensive or complicated assignments took their structures and goals from the contexts in which they occurred.

In this chapter we will examine the ways in which writing was successfully incorporated into the classrooms of the collaborating teachers. These include activities that the teachers were already using before the project began, as well as new activities introduced in the course of the research. The focus in the chapter will be on understanding the success of these activities — the principles underlying effective practice. In the following chapter, we will revisit these classrooms from a different vantage point, examining the interaction of these activities with the teachers' goals — including the circumstances in which a change in writing activities was but a symptom of a much more fundamental redefinition of teaching and learning.

Although the activities in these seven classrooms took many different forms, these forms served a limited number of functions:

1. To draw on relevant knowledge and experience in preparation for new activities

2. To consolidate and review new information and experiences

3. To reformulate and extend knowledge

All three are general pedagogical functions rather than unique functions of writing, but each provides a context within which writing activities can often find a comfortable home. Depending on the teachers' purposes, all three can be used primarily to evaluate students' knowl-

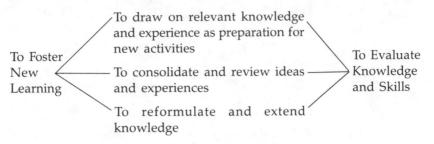

Figure 3. Purposes of writing in the classroom.

edge and skills or primarily to foster the development of new learning (see figure 3).

Writing to Draw on Relevant Knowledge

Classroom activities must begin somewhere, and most teachers develop their own favorite routines for stimulating students' interests, assessing (or reminding them of) what they already know, and focusing their attention in an appropriate direction. These are functions that appropriately structured writing tasks can fulfill — but only if the teachers believe that the students have relevant prior knowledge to draw upon in their writing.

When our collaborating teachers believed the students knew too little about the subject, they turned to lecture or demonstrations, rather than to student writing, as a way to begin. As we have seen, Kathryn Moss construed chemistry as a formal body of knowledge about which her students knew nothing. Given that belief, writing did not make sense as a preparatory activity at the beginning of a unit of study. During her participation in the project, she tried a freewriting activity before her students began a unit, but since she did not see evidence of the knowledge she sought, she never used that kind of activity again. She did develop a series of review-writing activities as preparation for quizzes, and these worked well for her because they were introduced at a point where students had some formal knowledge of chemistry on which they could draw.

In contrast, Janet Bush used freewriting activities (she called them "five-minute writing") to prepare her students even when they had little or no knowledge about a new topic. Although the students had trouble with such activities when they first encountered them, over time they learned to ask better questions — questions that helped them frame the new unit of work. The first such assignment dealt with crayfish:

> What do you know about crayfish? Write anything you can about crayfish, without worrying about the form of what you say. You can write a poem, you can write about nightmares involving crayfish, or you can write about what you'd like to know about crayfish.

Students were told that they had to keep writing for five minutes — even if all they did was write "I don't know anything about crayfish" over and over again. When we asked her what she had written for this assignment, Margaret, one of the case-study students, said she had written "just that I had never actually seen one. . . . I gathered from class what phylum they were from and all that stuff; that's about all I knew."

As they grew more familiar with this type of writing assignment, the students grew better at responding to it, learning to relate their comments to the more general context of biological study. Thus in response to a later assignment at the beginning of a unit on vertebrates, Margaret wrote: "What are vertebrates? Are they different from animals without backbones, because we've been doing invertebrates? What is their digestive system and nervous system like that are any different?" Although she had few answers, Margaret had begun to learn the kinds of questions she could profitably ask.

If Bush's use of preparatory writing helped students focus on relevant questions to frame their studies, Jack Graves saw such writing as primarily motivational. He described his use of assignments of this sort rather casually during our initial interview in November:

> I suppose you need to generate a little interest before you have them read literature. It's a natural thing for an English teacher to fall back on. It may not be in a history class or a biology class, but for an English teacher to say "Take out your pencil and address yourself to this idea," that's not unusual.

As we studied Graves's classroom, his initial casual comment turned out to be a very accurate reflection of his use of writing of this sort. Earlier in the year, for example, he had asked his students to complete an impromptu theme (he called it a "freewrite") on the topic of tattoos, before studying a poem about them. He was particularly pleased with this assignment, because it tapped into something the students felt strongly about initially. Students "can do very well on anything which is kind of an emotive, an immediate response. And then their writing is not phony at all. . . . Where the authentic voice gets lost is when writing about literature."

For Graves, the purpose of such preparatory writing was to stimulate students' interest; it was not an integral part of the literary study that followed. In his work on the project, he tried to use similar early writing activities as a lead-up to the final, formal essays that culminated each unit of study in his class. He was comfortable with such activities, though they never gained a very high priority among the competing demands for classroom time. For him, the study of literature involved students in both a "journey out of themselves" and a "journey in." The journey out of themselves involved coming to understand the relationships among ideas within a text, ideas that were broader and more important than students' individual experiences, but the journey in was dependent upon students' own ideas and experiences. Graves viewed the "journey in" that preparatory writing provided as secondary to the "journey out" that was at the heart of literary studies.

This differentiation was also evident in the collaboratively developed writing activities for a unit on *Great Expectations*; the activities began with a freewriting focusing on the question, "What should a good parent provide a child?" The freewriting began as a way to help students bring their personal experiences to bear on their reactions to Pip's early life, at the beginning of the novel. It was also meant as a lead-in to a second writing assignment, on Joe and Mrs. Joe as parents.

Graves introduced the freewriting on a Thursday, twenty-nine minutes into the period. As the students put away their grammar books, he wrote the question on the board. He told them to write approximately half a page, and that when they finished they could go on to their work for the next day. (In this case as in others, he used the term "freewriting" to describe an impromptu essay without a specified structure.) Most students wrote for about ten minutes and then moved on to their reading. Commenting on their involvement, Graves noted that if he were asked to write on such a topic, he would feel that he had to say something important. But he thought the students were comfortable with spontaneous writing precisely because they did not feel obliged to say things that were important. In his responses to what the students had written, he saw no need to make connections to the novel or to the substance of the follow-up assignment on Joe and Mrs. Joe.

The students in Graves's class reflected his distinction between the motivational, personal writing and the formal, text-based writing that he asked them to do. As Sandy, one of the case-study students, put it, in the freewritings "you can put your own thoughts, experience into it," whereas in the formal papers "you just write what was in the book, not really what you learned."

The freewriting assignment, then, worked because it was fully assimilated to the central concerns that governed Graves's teaching of literature. It fostered the "journey in" and "authentic voice" that he had come to expect from personal writing, stimulating interest and getting students involved before tackling the more significant work of the "journey out," a journey that would be constrained to the boundaries defined by the literary text.

Writing to Consolidate New Information

Many of the teachers found it difficult to use writing as a way to introduce new activities, because they felt that students would not know enough to have anything to write about. For these teachers, it was much easier to use writing as a way to help students review what they had learned. This review writing took a variety of forms, including log or journal writing, summarizing new material, note-taking, and study exercises. Reviewing new learning was one of the most frequent functions of writing in the participating classrooms. It played a particularly important role in the three science classes, each of which placed considerable emphasis on the learning of specific information.

The usefulness of writing in review became clear during our first year, in our work with Julian Bardolini. At the time we began our work with him, he was using note-taking and end-of-chapter study questions to serve review functions. In addition, he included some essay writing as part of end-of-unit exams. This combination of activities proved somewhat frustrating for both Bardolini and his students. He graded the end-of-chapter questions perfunctorily, and he never reviewed the notes at all. By the time students reached the unit exams, they were uncertain what he wanted. As Connie, one of the four case-study students in his class, put it in the interview cited in the previous chapter, "No one can usually fit it together."

Our collaboration with Bardolini focused on ways to help students "fit it together" by getting them to write about examination material before the in-class examination essays. The vehicle that worked best for this was the learning log, completed daily in class as a way for students to pull together in their own words what they had learned that day. At the beginning, because it was an unfamiliar activity, Bardolini introduced the log carefully. The students were given special notebooks to use for their learning logs, and wrote four questions on the inside cover as guides in responding to activities:

1. What was done?

2. What was learned?

3. What was interesting?

4. What questions remained?

On the day the notebooks were distributed, he also gave the students a page of sample entries, drawn from earlier studies of science classes (Applebee et al., 1984), as models of what their logs might contain.

When Bardolini introduced the learning logs, he ran into some initial problems. The lesson after which he had planned to introduce them ran longer than anticipated, leaving little time for the logs to be explained. This produced some confusion and frustration among the students, who were not sure what they were supposed to do or why they were supposed to do it. Explanations during later lessons, and supportive but directive comments in response to early entries, solved these problems. Bardolini had also begun by placing the log writings at the end of class, where they came in conflict with the reading of daily announcements — a ritual that had come to mean, "Class is over." In that context, the students did not take the logs seriously; in fact, most spent the log-writing time packing up their books and talking with neighbors. He solved this problem by rearranging classroom routines, moving the daily announcements to the beginning of the class and establishing an uninterrupted period for log-writing that was clearly separate from packing-up rituals.

The nature of the logs gradually evolved during the period Bardolini worked with the project. The initial entries were very short, often no more than a few sentences. Because he had little previous experience with logs, he brought the initial sets of entries to the project team to discuss how to encourage more fully elaborated responses. The following entries from the first day of the logs are typical both of student entries and of the responses with which Bardolini began:

> *Student entry:* Today we were lectured on nerve cells, kinds of neurons and neuron transmittors. The lecture was interesting, and I learned a lot about how we react to pain, pressure, and heat.
>
> *Teacher's response:* Susie, I am glad you found the lecture on nerve cells interesting. I'd like to read more of what you learned on reaction to pain, pressure, and heat.
>
> *Student entry:* We learned all about the neuron. The neuron has three parts, the dendites, the axon, the cell body.
>
> *Teacher's response:* Martin, this is a good way to start. Now what you need to do is write more — much more.

Bardolini used these as models at first, though he was still struggling to convert the new activity into practical classroom routines. Some of the students used the log as a way to vent their own frustrations with biology, and sometimes with the teacher, in a way that would not have been sanctioned in class: "Mr. Bardolini got sidetracked into talking about sex, but that seems to happen every day." Another commented, "I didn't like it at first, but I like it now because if Mr. Bardolini has done something in class I don't really like, I like putting it down here in the log ." Bardolini responded well to these criticisms, even commenting at one point, "I want them to write more than 'the lecture is boring.' I want them to tell me *why* it is boring; what I can do to *improve*." In spite of this tolerance, he gradually focused the logs more and more directly on the content his students had studied. Early in the process he suggested that the students use their class notes as further material to draw upon while writing the logs, clearly foreshadowing the later evolution of this activity.

One of the difficulties with the logs was in dealing with the team's suggestion that they should not be graded. This suggestion had emerged during one of the collaborative planning sessions, prompted by the sense that ungraded logs were most likely to be treated as a learning activity rather than part of the evaluation process. Bardolini soon found this approach uncomfortable and complained that he had "no sense" of how the students were reacting to the logs, because "I've asked them to do it; they want a grade, they'll do it." Some of the students clearly shared this perception, expecting to be graded on the logs in spite of the teacher's initial assurance to the contrary. Thus Max, one of the case-study students, confided, "I get the feeling it's going to be part of our grade, writing in the log. A big part." The interview continued:

> *Research assistant:* What gave you that feeling?
> *Max:* Just the way he always says, "Write in your log," and he makes it mandatory.
> *Research assistant:* Does that feeling affect the way you write in the log?
> *Max:* It tells me I should definitely write in it!

Later in the year Susan came to a similar conclusion: "I got a bad grade; I'm writing what he wants [now]."

We traced the continuing evolution of the learning logs in Bardolini's repertoire through interviews at the beginning and end of the next school year. During this next year, he extended the use of logs to all three of his general biology classes, convincing his department chair to purchase the necessary notebooks for all of the students (during the first year, the project had supplied the notebooks for the cooperating class). Bardolini structured the logs around the four guide questions, asking that students respond during the last five minutes of class, or if time ran out,

> ... These are obligations at home for five minutes — to think about what they did that period. ... The reason I wanted them to do this was that I feel they should get their things together that they learned. 'Cause a lot of them just come to class a week later and take a quiz or a test and never even look at their notes until they study for a test.

He began the second year still insisting that the logs were for the students' benefit and were not graded, but by the following June the activity had been fully assimilated into his general system of points. The logs were collected "two or three times each quarter," and the students received full points for doing the entries. The activity had become an expected part of the routine: "They know what they have to do and most of them accept it as a way of getting a good grade other than testing. ... [Doing the log] could guarantee a perfect score. They love it."

A year after we finished working with Bardolini, the learning logs had become a relatively stable part of his teaching routines, and his biggest concern was how to finance them the following year if the department chair balked at the continuing expense. (At $1.19 per bound notebook, the expenditure was not trivial.) His proposed solution was to divide the students' laboratory notebooks in half, keeping one half for the lab work and using the other half for the logs — thus having to provide two books only for students who wrote a lot.

The logs worked for Bardolini because he was able to adapt them to fit several crucial features of his teaching: (1) They served to review and reinforce difficult material on a regular basis, forcing students to review the notes that they otherwise seemed to ignore. (2) He was able to adapt them, through a system of points for completion of entries, to a general classroom economy that was evaluation-driven. (3) By collecting them only once a month or so and grading them on completion of entries, he was able to keep paper grading to a manageable level.

Review writing was also an important activity for all the other teachers we studied, in each case with its own necessary twists to help it work comfortably within each teacher's established routines. Naomi Watson, with her general concern for helping students organize and retrieve important information, included in her class routines a wide variety of review activities, ranging from study sheets focusing on particular readings to a daily journal introduced as a way to ensure systematic "filing" of information for later reference. Kathryn Moss, who relied on regular "refresher" sessions to remind students of what they knew before exams or quizzes, switched to five-minute review writing as a way to ensure that everyone was involved. Janet Bush, with her concern with concepts in biology, used informal note-taking, scientific logs, unit exams, and freewriting exercises to ensure that students were developing the needed base of information about biology. Jack Graves, who emphasized the "right" way to put ideas together, found review writing helpful as a way to check on whether students had done their assigned homework, a checking function fulfilled quickly by written responses to short-answer questions. Bill Royer and Jane Martin also used a variety of short-answer study sheets to review social studies material, but coupled this with summary writing and other extended review-writing exercises.

Writing to Reformulate and Extend Knowledge

The third major function of writing in the case-study classrooms reflected the use of language as a tool to reorganize and reflect upon what students knew or had learned. In such writing, students were asked to explore relationships among the concepts they had studied, developing classification systems, tracing cause and effect, explaining motivation, or speculating about future developments. All seven of the participating teachers valued such functions of writing, though they differed on how such purposes could be achieved with their students — and even on whether they could be achieved at all.

For our first example of how the teachers used writing to help students reformulate new understanding, we will look at Jack Graves's class in the midst of their study of *Romeo and Juliet.*

Juliet's Decision

Graves believed that his central task as a teacher of English and literature was the "putting together of ideas." At the same time, however, he felt it was important that his students learn how "to get it right the first time," and that to emphasize fluency before correctness would therefore work against students' best interests. This pairing of concerns led him to emphasize frequent writing within a highly structured format. He prepared students carefully, he said, suggesting the organization as well as the points that needed to be emphasized in a formal essay. He expressed some ambivalence about his approach:

More often than not I'm probably telling them what to say. That's bad 'cause I guess I shouldn't do that. No, it's not, and it's something I should do more of, laying the groundwork. . . . I go in two directions here. One is that I don't want to tell them what to say. And the other is that I want to give them some direction so they don't feel lost when they have to do it.

In his teaching, Graves preferred to err on the side of giving students more rather than less direction. His assignments typically provided the class with a thesis statement (and sometimes with complete opening and closing paragraphs) and a series of points from the text that illustrated the thesis.

We can see this process at work in a unit on *Romeo and Juliet,* which he concluded with a formal essay focusing on Juliet's decision to commit suicide in act 4. In developing this assignment, he began with a small-group activity in which he asked the groups to generate a series of alternative courses of action for Juliet when her parents try to arrange her marriage to Paris after she has already secretly married Romeo. For each alternative, the groups were to generate the pluses and minuses — why she might accept or reject it. The groups were puzzled by the assignment and had made little progress by the time he stopped the activity twelve minutes later.

The following day Graves used a class discussion to finish preparing the class for this essay. The interaction is interesting as an example of how he provided the class with the arguments to incorporate into their essays. He began by asking them to look at their notes from their small-group work, and then he helped them consider the implications of the alternatives in terms of what they knew about the play:

> *Graves:* Okay, uh, what was one of the alternatives you thought about?
>
> *Girl* [reads from her notes]: She could run away and live the rest of her life with Romeo.
>
> *Graves:* Okay, rather than take poison, why doesn't she just run away, straight away? All right, is there any advantage, can anyone think of any advantage of being thought dead? What's the advantage for people who do that?
>
> *Sandra:* They won't suspect that you're leaving.
>
> *Graves:* Right, they won't come look for you. They won't send somebody after you. Are the Capulets a powerful family?
>
> *Student:* Yeah.
>
> *Graves:* Yeah they have lots of servants and responsibility for this other [one word] for fear that there'll be civil war at the time. Okay, so they might not be martyrs then. Anybody disagree with that or see a problem with that?

Kathy: That they should remain with them.

Graves: Yeah, that's a pretty awful thing for a young girl. Maybe in the excitement of getting married, she's forgotten all about her family. If they knew this was going on they might miss her mother and father. Do you see any great affection between parents and child?

Girl: [a few words unclear]

Graves: No, I don't remember any place in the play that there's a tremendous amount of affection. Does Capulet address her in an affectionate way?

Girl: [a few words]

Graves: Yeah, when she comes back to her parents and tells them she's going to marry Paris. He calls her "my headstrong" and I think he's sort of teasing. How do you expect a relationship between a father and a daughter to look?

Girl: Close.

Graves: Real close. This is a matter, a truism. Girls get closer to their fathers. Okay, uh, so that's, that's interesting. And then what would she do? Where would they live? Do you think that Romeo's parents would support them?

Girl: No.

Graves: Can Romeo support himself?

Girls: No. Maybe.

Graves: How do you think a boy with a rich family got along in those days?

Girl: Got all his parents' money.

Graves: Exactly. He inherited it. In England the oldest son inherited all the property. And Romeo was the youngest son.

The discussion took five minutes to this point, and by then Graves had led students through the problems that would develop if Juliet were to elope with Romeo. The teacher then led the class through two similar explorations of the consequences of other alternatives that Juliet could have chosen. Finally, he brought them back to the paper that was due the next day:

Graves: Okay, I want you to begin, now we've got to think of some way, some beginning paragraph to include as many of these ideas as we can. How do we want to start out? What can we say as a preview? Now we've been talking about topic sentences or topic statements, statements that are going to tell the reader, uh, what to expect in the paper. So what is the reader gonna expect in your paper? Now I want you to come up with it. I've been giving it to you all along. Now I want you to come up with something. [pauses for one second] Well, what would . . . you don't need to come up with something that everyone could use. This is just going to be everyone's idea.

Sandy: [unclear]

Graves: Yeah, what she could have done instead, or why she did what she did do and why she did that. Do you think that's important to include in the paper?

Carolyn: Yeah.

Graves: Okay, I think it's important, yeah, because it's going to reinforce what you know about the play. So, how are we going to include what she actually did along with some of the things she might have done.

Nat: "Juliet has many options to take."

Graves: Okay. I like the word "options." That's a nice word. At what point are we at now? We're at the end of the play. We have to locate it in the action, the plot of the play. What point is she at in her options?

Girl: [unclear]

Graves: Okay, so, I think the important thing there is, that's good, we have to locate that in the plot. "After her father insisted that she do [aside to student, 'What?'] marry Paris, Juliet has several options." Okay, does that strike you as a way to, a way to go?

Girl: Yeah.

Graves: All right, fine.

At this point the students had a topic sentence and three well-developed examples to use for their rough drafts, which were due the following day.

Reflecting on this assignment a week later, Graves was pleased with the way it had helped the students understand the play. It was "a good assignment in that they were focused on the difficulty of the decision and it made them use their imagination, made them look into the different characters and see how they would have perceived different, alternate decisions." Sandy, one of the case-study students, agreed, commenting that writing about "the advantages and disadvantages of what she — Juliet — could have done gives you an idea of why she took the drug."

Create-an-Animal

Jack Graves's lesson on *Romeo and Juliet* is a good example of how a writing assignment and the activities that surround it can be used to reformulate and extend students' understanding of particular content, in this case of a literary text. For the next example, we will turn to Janet Bush's biology class and consider an assignment designed to move the students beyond the material they had studied to a point at which they could apply its underlying principles in new contexts. This assignment developed out of a collaborative planning session in which one of the team members suggested that the students might be asked to design their own creatures, drawing on their recent studies of organ systems and the evolutionary scale. Bush was pleased with the suggestion and fleshed out the particulars to fit with her general goals for the unit.

In its final form, the assignment took two days of class activity. On the first day, she provided a general overview of life processes and life systems, bringing together information that students had previously studied in separate units. She followed this with a problem-solving activity that focused on various life processes in the evolution of species and asked students to propose alternative solutions to those that nature had evolved. Students recorded their solutions in charts that she collected.

On the following day, she returned the charts with her comments and led the students into the writing activity itself: "Design an animal to live on land. Start with a chordate that lives in the water and decide what you have to do to get it to live on land." The students were required to discuss at least four organ systems (students could choose which) and to explain why they created the various features.

When a student asked how to start the paper, Bush kept the analytic task foremost: "I want my animal to look this way because. . . ." She suggested that students might want to include sketches of their new animals, along with explanations of their features and of the advantages these features might provide.

She was very pleased with this assignment and found that it brought a good response in all four of her biology classes. In her comments at the end of the project, she focused on this task as an example of the kind of writing she would like to emphasize more in the future:

> Assignments like the Create-an-Animal worked, worked really well — the kids really like it — and that's the most sophisticated level in Bloom's taxonomy . . .so I have to . . . I want to sit down and look at the different units that I teach and see if there isn't some more writing that I can incorporate at the evaluative level — after I've given the kids the groundwork.

Groundwork for the task was important: "It required them to take all their background knowledge — over a month's worth of stuff — and apply it to create a new thing." Bush also noted that students responded well to such tasks; of the things she asked them to do, it was "the stuff that they rankled about least."

The Create-an-Animal assignment was a relatively easy extension of the activities already well under way in Bush's biology classes. She placed a high value on teaching students to think creatively in science and was already using writing as an important tool in that process. The "What If" formula underlying the assignment is a powerful one, however, and is easily adapted to other topics and subject areas.

Practicing Conclusions

The process of drafting and revision can also be used as a powerful tool for helping students extend what they are learning. Kathryn Moss used it as she developed writing activities for her chemistry class. As we saw in the previous chapter, she was enthusiastic about the general idea of writing in science, but she was less than optimistic about the likelihood of success in chemistry class. One of the assignments that worked well in her class focused on students' problems in writing lab reports and was closely tied to her original goals. During our initial interview with Moss in November, she had commented on the problems that students had with formulating conclusions for their lab reports:

> *Moss:* They tend to wander, pulling everything in but the kitchen sink and not being very discriminating, and I think that's precisely the point of the synthesis of the lab, and for some kids I never quite get it across.
>
> *Research assistant:* When you say "not right" do you mean they're just missing the point of the lab?"
>
> *Moss:* They'll say, "You mix x with y and you get a precipitate"; that's not a conclusion. That's not a conclusion by my definition. I'm not getting that across even though I will sometimes read students' conclusions anonymously or make them up — or have the students make them up — and say in retrospect, "What do you think about this?" and they'll all laugh and say, "Aw, well. . . ." But some of them do equally foolish things to the point where some conclusions are gibberish. . . . And yet I consider that a very important part of the course and of the lab and of teaching the kids some scientific skills.

Although Moss felt that good conclusions should be limited to no more than two sentences, these two sentences were a critical part of reformulating and interpreting students' observations during the lab work.

In March, Moss returned to this problem and developed activities to help students write better conclusions. She began with an assignment sheet on practice conclusions, which she introduced with an analogy: In an article, the conclusion is the bottom line about which one asks, "Do I believe it?" In chemistry, the conclusion plays a similar role, providing a bottom line that should summarize what one can believe as a result of the experiment.

During the following week, when the assignment sheet was due, she continued with the work on conclusions. During the class, she developed several concepts relating to rates of reactions and then had students write quantitative statements about the relationships of rates of reactions in their current experiments. For the next twenty-six minutes she took the statements the students produced and worked with them on an overhead, helping the class revise them until the language was clear and the relationships were correctly stated. Then she asked the class to write practice conclusions for the lab.

In responding to the practice conclusions, Moss underlined flawed parts and occasionally wrote "good," but (as she noted) the process was very rapid. She was relieved that she did not need to make corrections, except for the occasional spelling error.

Two weeks later, she gave a second practice conclusion exercise. During our final interview with her, she described what happened:

> The writing assignment was done with the same constraints and rules as the first on practice conclusion writing. . . . I told them there were about two minutes left in the class period and if they'd do a practice conclusion, I would read it and give them feedback tomorrow and then time in class to fix up their conclusions in their notebooks if it was appropriate. And I told them that it would not be evaluated — that I didn't care whether they did it or not but that it was an opportunity for me to give them a little help in advance. . . . This was one of the most difficult labs that we do . . . and of the nineteen or twenty students that were there, fourteen submitted a practice conclusion with lots of scratched-out words and what not, and at least twelve of them remained after the bell rang working quietly — almost oblivious to the fact that the class was over. And I was taken aback that they were willing to do that.

Again, she found that she could read the practice conclusions quickly ("It took me minutes") and could see their answers evolving, as well as where they went a bit astray.

The case-study students found the practice conclusions helpful in different ways. Henry, who found conclusion-writing difficult, felt that Moss's work in class had been generally helpful, although he was unable to articulate the form the help had taken. Gina, who felt she understood the conclusions to begin with, thought the problem was semantic rather than conceptual. After the work in class, she concluded, "It's just how you word it. Most kids are probably putting in the right wording [now]."

The sequence of "practice conclusions" that Moss developed represented a form of draft-plus-revision before students recorded the final draft in their lab notebooks. Treating the conclusions as "practice" helped her focus on the content (which she saw as part of her job as a teacher of science) rather than the form (the job of the English teacher in her mind) and made them easy to review before returning to the students.

Impromptu Writing

In addition to formally structured assignments, many of the teachers used impromptu writing to encourage students to think about and reformulate material they were studying. Naomi Watson, who scheduled guest speakers at regular intervals, asked the students to write brief reaction papers after each talk. Jane Martin, who usually structured her assignments very thoroughly, began to use end-of-lesson assignments to help students make connections for themselves. Thus after a game that emphasized cooperation — and the penalties for everyone if people failed to cooperate — she passed out paper and announced:

> Now we are going to try to pull this together. We have just played a game. You have [also just] read a piece on life in a kibbutz. Write me two good paragraphs putting together the message of the game we played and the message of the article. Be sure to use examples from the article.

Although she still provided a certain amount of structure here (emphasizing two paragraphs and examples from the article), Martin treated this as an exploratory piece, allowing only ten minutes and marking the papers with a check or check-plus, rather than a grade. This brief writing activity helped the students draw out a set of connections that had been implicit in her planning but never brought to their attention.

In science, Janet Bush made similar use of impromptu responses in her five-minute format. After a film entitled *Hemo the Magnificent,* she gave her students very specific writing instructions:

1. What are the important points of *Hemo the Magnificent*?

2. What's the secret of sea water? Why does it have anything to do with blood?

While the first question served a simple reviewing function, the second forced the students to draw out relationships for themselves. Bush assured the students that they would receive full credit for making a sincere attempt, and in fact all received five points.

Evaluating Student Learning

The evaluation of student learning is a central pedagogical function in most classrooms, and those in our study were no exception. Most of the writing assignments the collaborating teachers ordinarily gave were designed in part to evaluate what students knew or had learned. When combined with the three pedagogical functions of writing we have been discussing so far in this chapter (preparing for new activities, reviewing, and extending concepts), evaluation takes very familiar forms: evaluation in preparing for new activities serves to *diagnose* student needs; evaluation in review writing serves to *assess* what students have learned; and evaluation in the context of writing to extend concepts reflects students' ability to *apply* what they know. Thus one of the teachers' persistent concerns as they developed new assignments for their classes was how these assignments should be evaluated. This concern had two components: what would constitute "good" work, and how to keep paper grading within reasonable limits. Without satisfactory answers to these two concerns, even our most enthusiastic teacher-collaborators quickly became uneasy. Like the activities themselves, the evaluative procedures varied from classroom to classroom. In turn, as we will see in the following brief accounts of each classroom, the evaluative procedures played a central and even controlling role in determining which writing activities would work best.

Julian Bardolini: Writing on the Point System

The classroom economy in Bardolini's class was driven by a point system. Every task that students were asked to do was given a point value, and final grades were based on the cumulative points earned during the grading period. We have already seen how this classroom economy interacted with the learning logs that eventually became a continuing part of his repertoire. At the beginning of the project, he tried to divorce the learning logs from the point system, emphasizing the value of the logs for their own sake. While fine in theory, in practice this approach made both teacher and students uncomfortable. The learning logs were not fully institutionalized until the following year, when they gained their own point value. Bardolini kept the consequent grading under control by collecting the logs only once a month and assigning points for completion of the activity rather than from a close or careful reading of the substance.

Other writing activities in his class also collected points — and the only activities that worked were those for which the points could be clearly defined. He was most comfortable when he could develop a "template" for the writing he assigned, a rubric that would give credit for particular items of information that could be expected at a given point in the writing. Speculative and open-ended assignments never worked well in his classroom, in large part because Bardolini could not predict what would come where in the responses — and hence could not develop a satisfactory rubric for them.

Jack Graves: Putting the Parts Together

As an English teacher, Graves had a good sense of what he was looking for in students' writing and was less concerned about the paper load that resulted; he perceived teaching students to write to be part of his job. As he described them in his initial interview with us, his goals for writing activities were broad: "having [the students] develop the skills, writing skills, being able to punctuate, to spell correctly, being able to illustrate by example or illustration, anecdote, some general statements, the ability to be interesting." He made regular use of peer editing groups to improve the mechanical aspects of students' writing before it was turned in; second drafts, a regular part of most assignments, focused on correcting mechanical errors the editing groups had caught. All assignments in his classes were graded and returned the following day, with separate grades for content and grammar.

In his classes, content was defined in practice as the development of a correct interpretation of the texts being read. One of the major values he saw in formal writing was that it helped students "decode" the language of the text and put it back together properly. The new assignments that worked best in Graves's classes were therefore those that let him judge the students' emerging interpretations. Assignments that led in other directions, such as the personal writing that preceded *Great Expectations*, were treated as motivational and never played a major role in his classroom.

Naomi Watson: Grading for Participation

In Watson's survival skills class, writing was a tool in constant use: it was the way that information was recorded and filed away until it might be needed. Writing in one form or another was required every day, and she was conscientious about checking this work: "I'm not going to correct everything but if I don't collect them they feel it's not important, so whenever, whatever it is, they just turn it in." Like Julian Bardolini, Watson assigned points for this work, requiring the students to keep logs in which they recorded the points "so they can see how they're progressing." Unlike Bardolini, however, she was very casual about the way points were assigned:

> Well, I have to admit it's very quick. It's whether or not they're complete. And whether or not they've gotten the gist of the lesson. And I'll tell them, "Hey, I'll spot check a lot. There may be a question on an evaluation sheet and that's it. And that's how you've gotten your points for that day."

Given the frequency with which she looked at student work, she kept the assignments simple and short, usually less than a page so that she could capture the gist of a response by scanning it quickly.

Watson's approach to evaluation was highlighted in one of the first assignments she developed during the project. The assignment began as part of a unit on banking; she was going to give the students an inaccurate bank statement and ask them to draft a letter to the bank pointing out the error and asking for a correction. As she worked with this task, she transformed it into a letter of complaint about a defective product. She used this letter as the end-of-semester examination, spending the first half hour taking the students through a worksheet on consumer rights and a model letter of complaint. Students then spent fifteen minutes to half an hour on the letter for the exam. In discussing the exam later, Watson said she had told the students that the letters would be graded as acceptable or unacceptable, "And so that's really pretty much the way I checked them." In looking through the exam papers, she made a special point of one by a girl who was a "poor student in lots of ways but she really came through on this assignment. . . . [For] a lot of this, all you had to do was almost copy what I said, but on the other hand, she did that."

Watson's approach to evaluation made it relatively simple for her to introduce new activities, as long as the writing that resulted would be relatively short and the students would at least be able to make an attempt at the task.

Janet Bush: Differentiated Evaluation

Of all of the teachers from subjects other than English, Bush had given the most thought to writing activities before the project began. To facilitate the different types of activities she assigned, she had two different approaches to evaluation: a credit-no-credit point system for brief assignments such as lab notebooks or logs related to work in progress and a regular grading system for summary writing at the end of a unit. Her major problem in evaluating writing was time, a problem that surfaced in our first interview with her. When asked about her interests in writing in biology, she replied:

> My first preference is to give them essay tests, [but] I almost exclusively don't do it any more because I have thirty-five kids in the classroom and my first concern as a teacher is to give them immediate feedback. When they take a test, I want to give the test back the next day and go over it and I can't do it [using essay tests] with thirty-five kids in each class.

She also noted that when she gave a writing assignment, she felt "compelled to correct spelling and grammar."

Bush expressed similar problems with time in her use of logs as a way for students to keep track of their observations over a period of several weeks, synthesizing personal reactions with their records of what they had seen. Although she valued this activity and reduced the amount of grading by giving points for just completing the logs, she used logs for only three weeks of the year: "I can't justify incorporating [any more than that] in biology, because I have so much other material to cover."

She was comfortable evaluating open-ended material and had well-rehearsed procedures for dealing with work in progress as well. It was relatively easy for her to develop new writing activities, but only as long as paper-grading time could be kept to a minimum. In the assignments she developed during the project, this meant focusing on the content of the students' writing rather than the spelling and grammar and keeping the overall length of any assignment relatively short.

Kathryn Moss: Quizzes and Extra Credit

Moss's evaluation system was similar to Bush's — in-class writing was treated as a quiz and graded; homework and extra-credit assignments were worth points for completion. Also like Bush, Moss felt obligated to correct any work that she collected. She described this in her final interview with us:

> I was always hung up on the fact that if I made somebody write something down then I was obligated to play science teacher and English teacher and whatever — that I could not allow anything to be returned to them that did not have points on it and that did not have comments regarding grammar and spelling because I didn't want anyone to think that I accepted misspelled words and bad grammar, that I didn't know better.

Although we only gradually became aware of it, this attitude played a significant role in the success of the activities Moss developed during the project. For example, she found it difficult to work with freewriting activities in which students explored new material in class. Although she tried such writing on several occasions, in each case she found it awkward to deal with the papers. As a result, she simply threw some assignments away.

The activities that were successful worked in part because they were easily adapted to Moss's evaluation routines. She had little trouble with more formal writing given for extra credit or homework (simply awarding points for its completion) or with writing completed in class but not collected (the series of review-writing activities that became a permanent part of her teaching repertoire). She also had little trouble with the practice conclusions discussed earlier, which she did collect and read but treated as drafts to be incorporated into the final versions of the lab reports, rather than as work that had to be separately evaluated. Her success with the practice conclusions led her to rethink the need to correct mechanical errors on work in progress:

> I've decided that that isn't really important; . . . if the students are trying to write their thoughts down, they can't do both things at once — in one shot — and that as long as we all agree ahead of time it's okay if it's not said in the best form and if it's not grammatically clear or if the spelling is a little off. We're really interacting in ideas and we're not going to worry about those other things.

Jane Martin: Getting It Right

Martin's major concern in her social studies class was that the students should be successful at what they did. She sought to ensure this by providing a highly structured working environment for them, one where right answers would be clear and students could easily succeed. At the beginning of the project, more than 90 percent of the written work in her classroom involved worksheet activities (true-false, matching, and fill-in-the-blank exercises) in which the students did not have to compose extended text at all. Grading for such exercises was simple, since each response was either right or wrong.

Longer assignments were given letter grades, but even in these Martin kept the standards for success simple. One of the collaboratively developed assignments in her class, for example, evolved as part of a unit on India. She asked her students to write a letter to a friend after a trip there:

> Imagine you have been on an all-expense paid, unchaperoned trip to India. You saw sights, heard sounds, and did things that thrilled your innermost soul. . . . As a good friend, you are going

to write me a letter telling me about all the things you have experienced. Be original, be clever. Make me wish I were there instead of you.

Martin structured this assignment to ensure the students' success: the letter format was familiar, and the assignment invited narrative storytelling rather than analysis and argument. Her evaluative criteria were simple, too: she counted the number of items that were specifically Indian and based her letter grades on the totals.

Her writing assignments, then, worked well as long as the form and content were clear and the right answer could be kept sharply in focus. As assignments became more open-ended, her discomfort grew — although, as we will see in the next chapter, over the course of the project she came to value such assignments more and struggled to find ways to evaluate them.

Bill Royer: Keeping to the Task

Of the seven teachers, Royer had the least clearly articulated set of criteria for evaluating student work. In discussing his teaching during his initial interview with us, he voiced concerns with fundamental concepts rather than collections of facts:

> I will choose questions that I think get at certain issues to see if they've read enough in the chapter to understand the concept. I've always been a person in the social studies who is not concerned with dates and this kind of thing — but more with the cause and effect relationships — why things happen as they happen. On the Civil War final, for example, will be the obvious question, "Could the Civil War have been avoided?"

Despite these concerns, Royer's actual grading practices emphasized completion of the work assigned. Students usually received a grade on a twenty-point scale, with few comments beyond an occasional "good." Long answers tended to get higher grades, almost irrespective of content. The few criteria that he did use consistently were isolated rules of good writing that were easy to apply to student work. He would not accept papers that began, "In this paper I am going to write about . . . ," for example, insisting instead on "some kind of hypothesis statement at the beginning." Nor would he accept papers that strayed off topic: "No matter how much you write, if you don't address the specific issues, you don't get credit."

All work was graded in class, however, and this proved to be a significant factor in the kinds of writing that functioned well in his class. He was uncomfortable with assignments that were meant as work in progress rather than as finished products for evaluation. As he put it in our last interview with him, "When you say it's a check-off assignment, the kids say, 'Oh, okay,' and you get a laid-back attitude and you have to guard against that sort of thing."

The Thinking That Writing Evokes

During the second year of the study, we also gathered think-aloud protocols from the case-study students as they completed their regular classroom assignments. Forty-seven protocols were collected in all, sampling the variety of activities in the six classrooms. These protocols provided another view of the writing activities and allowed us to ask whether the students' approaches to the tasks in fact led to the kinds of thinking implicit in our characterization of the tasks as "preparatory," "review," and "reformulation."

To examine this, we used Langer's (1986a, 1986b) system of protocol analysis, involving segmentation of the protocols into communication units and categorizing each communication unit to reflect the kinds of manipulation and the specific concerns of the writer at that time. The categories we used are listed in table 4; Appendix 1 summarizes the procedures for applying the scoring system.

A number of categories in Langer's system reflect different aspects of the writers' focus on conceptual relationships and structure within the body of information being dealt with, versus a more narrow focus on specific items of content. Comments categorized as *hypothesizing* reflect the writers' predictions about the tasks they are immersed in; such comments imply a sense of the structure of the whole and also imply a process of building relationships among the ideas being developed. *Questioning*, in contrast, reflects a less structured approach without the clear sense of direction that hypotheses embody. *Meta-comments* include statements about the process as a whole; in the protocols from the present study, they tended to reflect puzzlement about the task. *Using schemata* involves simple statements drawn from the students' knowledge of subject-area content or personal experience. *Other operations* combine a variety of low-frequency functions, including citing evidence, making assumptions, validating previous hypotheses, evaluating, and reading from related materials. We also categorized each statement as *global* (pointed toward the text or process as a whole) or *local* (pointed toward specific parts of the evolving text or process of writing it).

The results from these analyses, for the assignments that were used as preparatory activities, for review, and for reformulation and extension

Table 4

Characteristics of Think-Aloud Protocols by Purpose of Writing

	Preparation (n = 10)		Review Restricted (n = 5)		Summary (n = 14)		Reformu- lation (n = 18)	
	M	(SD)	M	(SD)	M	(SD)	M	(SD)
Communication units	39.7	(25.7)	42.6	(17.9)	35.7	(44.4)	45.5	(34.2)
Units occurring before writing (%)	9.4	(12.7)	6.7	(6.9)	9.4	(18.8)	24.3	(29.4)
Reasoning operations (%)								
Hypothesizing	6.9	(7.6)	3.3	(3.6)	3.0	(3.7)	15.8	(14.5)
Questioning	15.9	(15.8)	9.1	(6.4)	16.7	(13.4)	7.8	(5.7)
Making metacomments	10.2	(9.7)	12.3	(8.9)	4.4	(5.7)	4.2	(4.4)
Reading own writing	7.7	(10.6)	0	—	5.0	(7.1)	5.4	(7.5)
Using schema:								
Content	48.6	(15.8)	58.3	(9.3)	59.7	(19.0)	50.5	(20.2)
Personal	8.4	(14.7)	9.3	(9.4)	2.5	(4.7)	0.1	(0.6)
Other operations	2.2	(2.6)	7.6	(8.1)	8.8	(12.1)	16.2	(20.8)
Global (versus local) comments (%)	2.9	(5.1)	2.9	(3.4)	7.8	(15.5)	12.0	(21.5)

of new ideas, are summarized in table 4. Review writing is subdivided into (1) restricted writing activities in which students responded to two or more specific questions and (2) summary tasks that stemmed from a single broad prompt (for example, "Write everything you can remember about vertebrates").

The four types of tasks led to writings of similar average lengths and to similar average numbers of communication units in the protocols. However, some interesting differences in the types of comments included in the protocols reflected differences in what the students were led to do in response to the various tasks.

Looking at patterns across categories, we can see that activities meant to help students reformulate and extend concepts led to the most concern with structure and relationships among ideas, while the review-writing tasks led to the least concern. Hypothesizing, for example, was most frequent in reformulation activities (16 percent of the units) and least frequent in the two review-writing activities (3 percent). Conversely, questioning was least frequent in reformulation (8 percent of the units) and most frequent in summary-writing and preparatory activities (16 to 17 percent).

Concern with a sense of the whole is also reflected in the proportion of the comments that writers made before actually beginning to write. Reformulation seems to have required considerably more thinking before writing (fully 24 percent of the protocol comments, compared with 7 to 9 percent for the other activities).

Patterns for global versus local comments were consistent with these trends, indicating that the writing activities categorized as demanding extension and reformulation did in fact lead to more concern with larger units than is apparent in the other tasks. Review activities, in contrast, led to a greater focus on specific content and less on global concerns, relying on the original material to give shape and coherence. Preparatory activities led to a more diffuse pattern, with considerable questioning and metacommentary and some drawing on personal experience.

Discussion

What kinds of writing "work" in academic classrooms? We found that this question cannot be answered at the level of particular writing activities. Each of the classrooms developed its own unique configuration of writing assignments, a configuration that reflected the individual teacher's subject-specific goals, general constructs of teaching, and methods of evaluation. At the level of the broader functions that writing can serve, however, the answer is easier. The types of activities that we observed in each of the classrooms are summarized in table 5. Writing to review and writing to reformulate and extend ideas and experiences found some place in each of the classrooms; preparatory writing, either to motivate students or to draw on their prior knowledge, found a place when the teachers believed that the students knew enough about the topic to write at all.

Writing to evaluate learning was also universal, though what that meant in practice took different forms in each of the seven classrooms. In each class, evaluation was tied very closely to the teacher's central concerns, and changes in writing activities (including the introduction of some writing activities reflecting work in progress) were shaped by how well those activities could be accommodated to the evaluation system. Activities that could not be accommodated to the evaluation system either failed in their initial introduction or were quietly dropped from the teacher's repertoire.

Our examination of think-aloud protocols gathered while students were completing these activities suggests that in fact the preparatory,

Table 5

Writing Activities Used by the Seven Teachers

	Pedagogical Function		
Teacher	Preparatory	Review	Reformulation
Graves	Impromptu writing	Study sheets	Impromptu essays Formal essays
Watson	Freewriting	Freewriting Study sheets Letters Daily journals Note-taking	Reaction papers Study sheets Letters
Martin	Personal experience Freewriting	Study sheets Freewriting Letters Journals[a] Summaries Note-taking Personal reaction[a]	Impromptu essays Formula paper Letters Unit papers
Royer	Freewriting[a]	Summaries Study sheets Daily logs[a]	Formal essays Outline of argument Project work Reaction papers
Moss	Review writing Freewriting[a]	Review writing Freewriting[a] Journals[a] Note-taking	"What if . . ." papers Practice conclusions
Bush	Freewriting Impromptu writing	Unit essays Impromptu writing Informal notes Scientific logs	Unit essays Impromptu essays "What if . . ." papers
Bardolini	—	Note-taking Learning logs Essay exams Lab reports Restricted writing	Focused logs[a] Learning logs[a] Extended essays[a]

[a] Activities perceived as unsuccessful by the teacher.

review, and reformulation activities did lead to different patterns of thinking about the material. Writing to reformulate led to a greater concern with structure and with relationships among ideas, whereas review writing led to more emphasis on the particular content.

Although we have focused on patterns in individual classrooms, the results are consistent with our earlier findings of subject-area differences in the goals and nature of effective writing activities. In the science classes, the writing activities that the teachers developed most easily were those that seemed likely to reinforce learning of a broad base of factual information — a base that the teachers perceived as necessary for more sophisticated inquiry. Two of the science teachers (Bush and Moss) also successfully developed writing activities that emphasized such inquiry, once the necessary base of information was in place. Although Bardolini said that he valued such inquiry, he was never able to incorporate it successfully into his classroom routines.

The English and social studies teachers, on the other hand, began with a greater emphasis on underlying concepts. It was easier for them to develop new writing activities that emphasized reformulation and extension of previous learning. In these activities, the emphasis was on the structure of the argument more than on the specific information — though accuracy in supplying the supporting detail was still critical to successful performance.

In our thinking about the successful activities, one of the themes that has emerged is the process of reinterpretation and reconstruction that the teachers went through before presenting a new activity to their classes. The collaboration with the project team provided new ideas and new perspectives on old approaches, which the teachers then had to claim ownership for in a process of transformation and elaboration. Often, the activities we observed in the classroom bore little resemblance to the activity that had taken initial shape in our joint planning sessions. Conversely, when the teachers did take other people's activities ready-made, the activities were likely to fail. It seemed that when the teachers understood and believed in an activity, they were comfortable modifying it to achieve their own goals. When they did not fully understand or accept it, on the other hand, they were less able to mold it to suit their own purposes.

Certain generic activities proved especially attractive and adaptable, being redefined by each teacher even if the label remained the same. Freewriting was one such activity, emerging in one or another classroom as a preparatory activity, a way to review and rehearse previous learning or a way to reformulate and extend new ideas. (In several of the classrooms, freewriting was defined to include any less-formal or impromptu writing; the label may have served to sanction the lack of structure in otherwise highly structured learning environments.) Journals or learning logs were similarly flexible, becoming whatever each teacher wanted to make of them. Flexibility seemed desirable rather than problematic; such activities worked because they were easily adapted to differing contexts of teaching and learning.

At the same time, this very flexibility contributed to a growing terminological confusion: freewriting was not freewriting was not freewriting, and journals were not journals were not journals. This led to a situation in which it was very easy for us to misunderstand the teachers and for them to misunderstand one another — all enthusiastically supporting differing concepts of learning that coexisted under the same label. This terminological confusion is not specific to the project but reflects the wide variety of interpretations that have developed in the general field of writing. The differences serve to remind us of the variation in course-specific and teacher-specific goals. Different ways of thinking undergird our professional agendas and are reflected in the nature of the writing assignments that work best in each class.

5 Teachers in Transition: Changing Conceptions of Teaching and Learning

The studies reported so far have emphasized the most obvious changes that were taking place in the classrooms in the study. Together with the seven teachers, we developed a variety of new writing activities and explored in some detail how they fit into the ongoing stream of classroom activity. Some activities worked well while others did not, and these successes and failures became more predictable as we came to understand the concepts of teaching and learning at work in each classroom.

There is another perspective to take on our data, however, and that is to look more closely at the teachers themselves as individual professionals in the midst of changing their approaches to teaching. We began the project with a particular set of concerns and predispositions, which we have sketched in the introductory chapter. We were concerned with writing as a tool for learning, a context within which students could explore new ideas and experiences. In particular, we were concerned with what are often called "process" approaches to learning, where ideas are allowed to develop in the learner's own mind through a series of related, supportive activities; where taking risks and generating hypotheses are encouraged by postponing evaluation; and where new skills are learned in supportive instructional contexts.

In classrooms adopting these approaches, much of the work that students produce reflects this process of instruction, rather than final drafts to be submitted for evaluation. In such contexts, we have argued, students have the best chance to focus on the ideas they are writing about and to develop more complex thinking and reasoning skills as they explain and defend their ideas for themselves. Everyone in the current project — teachers as well as university-based researchers — began the project convinced of the value of such goals in academic learning and committed to exploring what would happen when process-oriented writing activities were embedded within the subject-area curriculum.

When we look at the results of our project from this perspective, they highlight the fact that process-oriented approaches are not simply

69

an alternative way to achieve subject-area goals. Instead, when these approaches are implemented most effectively, they bring with them a fundamental shift in the nature of teaching and learning. Rather than augmenting traditional approaches to instruction, in a very real sense such approaches undermine them — or are undermined in turn by the goals and procedures of more traditionally oriented approaches to teaching.

Thus the project led to substantial change in patterns of activity in almost all of the classrooms. In some of the classrooms, this change in activities reinforced the patterns of teaching and learning that were already in place at the beginning of the project. In others, it led to a major realignment in the teachers' goals. In the present chapter, we will explore the nature of this realignment in those classrooms where it did occur, as well as the factors that led some teachers and not others to adopt such changes.

To examine these issues, we looked at the data we had gathered — including analyses of interviews, planning sessions, and classroom observations — focusing on the teachers' concepts of teaching and learning and how these changed across the months we worked together. We studied teachers in transition, as they were in the process not only of developing new classroom activities, but also of developing new ways to conceptualize student learning in their subject areas. Using data from analyses of student interviews, think-aloud protocols, writing samples, and observations of behavior in class, we also examined the students' ways of thinking about their course content in response to the writing activities their teachers assigned. Thus we were able to examine the results of teacher change — the ways the teachers changed their conceptions of teaching and their uses of writing and how these changes affected the nature of learning while students were engaged in the academic tasks.

Changes in the Teachers' Approaches

If we look just at the activities the seven teachers used in their classrooms, we find that by the end of the project six of the seven had changed the activities they assigned, incorporating more (and more varied) writing activities than they had used in the past. (Only Bill Royer, with a curriculum constrained by an existing set of highly structured activities, seemed essentially unaffected by his participation.) As we saw in the previous chapter, these new activities fulfilled a variety of classroom functions, serving to motivate or prepare students for new work, to review material previously studied, and to reformulate and extend students' knowledge and experience. The activities often took forms familiar from the process-oriented teaching literature, including freewriting activities, journals, personal responses to new experiences, and some drafting and revision.

We were aware that such activities may affect learning in two ways: they may provide more effective techniques for achieving specified curriculum goals, and they may also lead to changes in the nature of the learning that is taking place. The design of our project, which included regular interviews with case-study students as well, as the analysis of samples of all students' work, allowed us to examine directly the students' patterns of learning in response to their teachers' approaches.

Purposes for Writing

We have already commented on the central role that evaluation played in determining how easily new activities could be assimilated into the classrooms in the project. Evaluation was also important in shaping the nature of students' engagement in classroom activities. In particular, when students assumed that an assignment would be evaluated, they were likely to treat it as a display of what they had already learned: they would present their ideas carefully and fully, but were likely to stay close to the known and the familiar. On the other hand, when they assumed that the writing was part of an ongoing instructional dialogue, they were more likely to use it to explore new ideas — taking more risks and accepting more failures.

To examine this aspect of student learning more systematically, the writing samples collected in the project classrooms were rated for audience, using a category system developed in earlier projects (see Applebee, Langer, et al., 1984, Appendix 1; Britton et al., 1975). This system distinguishes among four audiences for school writing: self, teacher as part of an instructional dialogue, teacher as examiner, and wider audience. Each writing sample was categorized by two independent raters, with a third rating to reconcile disagreements. There was 88.2 percent exact agreement between pairs of raters in categorizing the audience for the 743 writing samples analyzed.

The results for assignments completed at different points in our work with the teachers are presented in table 6. For teachers who began focusing more on the changes and growth in the ideas their students were writing about rather than solely on the accuracy of the information in a finished paper, we would expect to find a decrease

Table 6

Teacher-as-Examiner in the Eight Classrooms

| | Mean Percentage of Student Papers (*n* of assignments) | | |
| | | New Assignments | |
	Old Assignments	Early	Late
Year one			
Martin	100 (2)	55 (5)	75 (4)
Bardolini	88 (2)	58 (7)	89 (7)
Year two			
Martin	98 (3)	73 (3)	39 (3)
Royer	93 (3)	77 (2)	93 (3)
Graves	73(17)	70 (4)	90 (6)
Watson	65 (5)	72 (4)	56 (4)
Bush	93 (5)	58 (5)	70 (2)
Moss	92 (2)	50 (2)	67 (3)

Note: The table is based on 743 samples of student writing in response to 103 different assignments. Since unequal numbers of papers were collected for each assignment, tabled percentages are weighted so that each assignment counts equally in the average.

in the amount of writing addressed to the teacher-as-examiner. Many of the classrooms showed such a shift away from the teacher-as-examiner during their initial participation in the project. However, four of the teachers reestablished previous patterns of evaluation as they became more comfortable and familiar with the activities they were developing. With time, four of the teachers almost completely incorporated the new activities into their previous instructional routines, and their students' papers continued to be addressed to a teacher-as-examiner. The classrooms of Bush, Moss, and Martin showed a continuing decline in the proportion of the writing addressed to an examining audience. These changes were reflected as well in the student interviews and the observers' interpretations of the activities they were watching. In these classrooms, students began to use writing more as a tool for exploring new learning and less as a demonstration of what they had already learned. In the other four classrooms, the outward form of the activities changed, but the nature of the students' participation remained the same.

The explanation of this outcome has three parts, each of which will be explored in turn. Together, they form not only an explanation of what happened in the present study, but also a definition of the challenges to any program that seeks to achieve fundamental reform of current classroom practice.

1. When teachers develop new approaches, they interpret them on the basis of their own notions of teaching and learning. As a result, it is relatively easy to introduce new activities.

2. Major reforms in instruction may carry with them new definitions of what it means to teach and learn. If these reforms are adopted fully, they will lead to fundamental changes in teachers' notions of teaching and learning in their subject areas.

3. This will happen, however, only when teachers develop new ways to evaluate student progress that are consonant with the new approaches; otherwise, the teachers' new concepts will be undercut by inappropriate criteria for evaluation.

yes!

Assimilation of New Activities

One of the most consistent processes at work throughout the project was one in which approaches and activities that arose in the collaborative planning meetings were elaborated and reinterpreted while the teachers made them their own. In the previous chapter, we argued that this process of reinterpretation was necessary if the teachers were to claim ownership for what they were doing and ultimately to have any chance of success with the new activity. This process was also a primary mechanism for ensuring that the new activities supported and reinforced the teachers' own general goals and specific classroom routines.

We can see this process at work in Julian Bardolini's classroom. His central concern as he planned and carried out his classroom activities was the need to provide his students with a broad base of information about biology, and his role as a teacher was one of providing that information. Because the textbook was difficult and the information complex, he spent his lessons re-presenting the information and testing (in several formats) to see what the students had managed to learn. As we saw in the previous chapter, during the project Bardolini developed a learning log activity as a way for students to consolidate and reformulate what they had learned during a lesson. He was enthusiastic about the learning logs and incorporated them fully into his regular classroom routines. A year after his involvement in the project, he was still using the logs.

His use of the logs, however, was quite different from the uses usually suggested in the literature on the teaching of writing. In the literature, and indeed in the initial discussions in the collaborative planning meetings, the logs were discussed as providing students with the opportunity to synthesize and react to what they were learning, an opportunity to focus on their ongoing learning rather than on what they had already learned. Although Bardolini voiced agreement with these goals, they did not fit particularly well with his concern to convey the basic information of biology, and over time he redefined the logs to better fit his own purposes. Gradually, the emphasis shifted toward evaluation of what the students had learned from each lesson; the logs became an effective way to check on what they knew.

The process of assimilation is particularly evident in our analysis of the case-study students' entries in their logs. We collected sample entries at various times and analyzed the audience for whom the students were writing: themselves, their teacher as part of an ongoing instructional dialogue, their teacher in the role of examiner, or a wider audience.

The results were quite dramatic. In January, when Bardolini first introduced the logs, 57 percent of the students used them primarily as a way of exploring new ideas, casting the entries as part of an instructional dialogue. By March, the activity had begun to be assimilated to his usual approaches: 63 percent of the entries were addressed to the teacher-as-examiner. By May, entries addressed to the examiner had risen to 83 percent. The students sometimes reflected this orientation quite directly in their comments during our interviews with them. Connie, one of the case-study students, gave her impression of having been asked to write an entry in her log: "Today we had a pop quiz."

In this way, the science logs became an activity well suited to Bardolini's needs; they gave him a new and systematic way to sustain his focus on accurate learning of the substance of biology. He could do this because it was possible for him to redefine what the logs meant and how they would be used so that they would reinforce rather than subvert his own emphases in his teaching.

We can see a similar principle at work in the case of Kathryn Moss and her eleventh-grade chemistry class. Her view of science teaching emphasized the process of inquiry within the bounds of her course content. To undertake such inquiry, however, the students needed a base of information, and, in chemistry at least, providing that base of information was Moss's primary agenda. As we have seen, she was open-minded but skeptical about the value of writing in chemistry, viewing her subject as "formally structured" and the students "not into the point where they are putting creative writing into the course."

She commented in our initial interview, "I don't see a good way to get more writing from them, even though I think it is important." In the past she had tried journal writing, but had given it up because the students' responses were "superficial."

At the beginning of the project, Moss concentrated on activities that would be simple and useful and that would build on procedures already in place. During the collaborative planning sessions, she developed a series of review activities in which students spent about five minutes writing "everything they knew" on the topic they had been studying. She was excited about this "freewriting" activity because she recognized its usefulness in focusing her review lessons and in gaining individual participation; and this perception was reinforced by spontaneous comments from students about how helpful they, too, found the activity. These tasks also worked well for her because they required no correction or followup.

Once she had developed a notion of review writing, Moss incorporated it into her standard repertoire and began to explore several variations on it. In the earliest versions, the students' freewriting was followed by class discussion, with important points being summarized on an overhead projector. Later, she began to use review-writing tasks to focus students' attention before their quizzes (which came as often as twice a week), as the basis for class discussion, as a prelude to homework assignments, and by the end of the year as "open book" notes that pupils could refer to during the quizzes that followed. Although she checked all of the other work in her class, she read none of these review writings, which formed the basis of many lively discussions.

One of the most interesting aspects of Moss's use of review writing was the extent to which she came to take it as a matter of course. After the first month, she never discussed her plans for such writing with the project team or even mentioned them as part of the writing she was doing: they had become *hers* rather than *ours*. During the remainder of our work with her, one or another variation of review writing took place in over a quarter of the classes we observed, always without her thinking to mention it to us in advance.

Review writing worked well in Moss's classroom because it served a function she valued — preparation for quizzes — and did it better than the activities she had used to accomplish this in the past. As it evolved over time, review writing did not supplant class discussion as a preparatory activity, but it did serve as a way to enrich the discussions that followed and to ensure that everyone was involved. Because it was a preparatory activity, she was willing to postpone evaluation, allowing the students to use these brief writings as a way to review and consolidate what they knew. Moss quickly claimed review writing as her own rather than as a project activity, in part because it was fulfilling her own goals so well.

The Curriculum as a Set of Particular Activities

There was one exception to the general pattern of easy assimilation of new activities to old patterns of instruction. This occurred in Royer's class, where the curriculum was defined in terms of a particular and long-standing set of activities.

In his twenty-five years of teaching, he had developed a comfortable pattern for his classes. Early in his career, he had become a firm believer in the use of simulation games to teach history and had developed a detailed curriculum based entirely on a variety of simulation activities. Although he professed to value student opinions and to structure his classes around inquiry approaches, over time the particular activities he used had come to be valued in their own right. Progress in his classes was evaluated primarily on the basis of having completed each activity; neither the complexity of the response nor the degree of engagement seemed to figure highly. Because of this, Royer found it exceedingly difficult to incorporate any new writing activities into his classroom routines. New activities were threatening on two levels: they posed problems for evaluation, and they threatened to displace his well-established routines. As a result, though Royer was always cooperative and congenial in his work with us, he is the one teacher whose teaching seems to have been, in the long run, unaffected by our collaboration. He found it difficult to find space in his curriculum to experiment with new activities, and those he did try were quickly if quietly dropped.

Changing Conceptions of Teaching and Learning

The changes that took place in some of the classrooms were considerably more fundamental than those we have been discussing so far. Rather than simply assimilating new activities to ongoing patterns of teaching and learning, in these classrooms the patterns of teaching and learning themselves began to change.

Emphasizing Students' Thinking

In Bush's class, such changes occurred very quickly. She began the project convinced of the importance of teaching students to think for themselves as part of the process of scientific inquiry. She was also convinced of the role that writing could play in supporting such thinking, but she was constrained because of the time that the activities would consume. As she developed techniques for blending writing activities more easily into her ongoing work, she placed a gradually increasing emphasis on activities that gave students the opportunity to engage in extension and reformulation of what they were learning. Over time, her role in providing information dwindled away, replaced by her newly strengthened role in eliciting and supporting students' own thinking.

Moss's uses of writing in chemistry led to a slower but more extensive reconceptualization, as she came to recognize that her students were capable of a level of scientific thinking that she had not thought possible. We have already seen that her review-writing activities worked because she could assimilate them to her previous understanding of what mattered in learning chemistry. Broadening her teaching repertoire to include other kinds of writing activities was more difficult, because she saw them as involving "creative" thinking, and there was no place for creative thinking in students' initial learning of chemistry. As a result, she considered her first attempts at introducing writing in other ways to be dismal failures: completion rates were low, and when students did hand their work in, she did not know what to do with it. In most cases she procrastinated, and eventually threw the work away.

Moss's views of science learning did value hypothesis development and prediction, though she was doubtful that her students (in contrast to the biology classes she sometimes taught) knew enough chemistry to undertake such activities. This view provided her with a context for introducing the first successful longer writing assignment in her chemistry class, asking students to invent a new element and predict its behavior given its hypothetical structure. She was excited about the idea, but also feared that it would be too difficult for the students. Rather than abandoning it, she used the collaborative planning sessions to develop some ways to give the assignment more flexibility. She decided to set it as a homework assignment, where there would be "less pressure around the writing." (Homework assignments were usually given full credit for an honest attempt at the assignment, rather than being graded.)

Her initial hesitation changed to enthusiasm as she worked out the details of the assignment. By the time she presented it to the class, she told them she would love to make it a test, but did not want it to take on "ominous dimensions." Instead, she assigned it as homework, adding, "The best part is that you cannot open up a book and look any of this up." The assignment was going to require the students' own ideas.

To prepare the students, Moss spent fifteen minutes in class explaining what was required and reminding them of specific scientific information they would need to consider. ("If the atomic number were 118, it would look like an inert gas.") With this preparation, students responded well to the assignment, though they were aware of the difference between it and most of their other writing in chemistry. As Gina, a case-study student, explained in commenting on the assignment later, "It wasn't that hard; but it was hard because it wasn't like a definite yes or no answer. It wasn't yes, it's right; no, it's not right."

Moss's first comment to us after she had read the papers was, "This writing stuff is kinda fun." Though it had taken two months of daily collaborative planning to get this far, the assignment marked a major turning point in her ability to use writing as part of her science class. She had many failures as well as successes in the remaining months of the project, but she was not deterred by the failures. She had come to believe that even in chemistry it was possible to teach the students to think for themselves, to develop "thought processes such as hypothesis development, conclusions, and designing experiments." These processes were a central part of her understanding of the scientific process, but she had not thought she could help her chemistry students learn to do them. This perception did not replace her original concerns with providing a solid base of information from which her students could work, but it represented a significant extension and redefinition of what would count as "knowing" in her classrooms. And this redefinition was a direct result of her experience with a writing activity that she did not assimilate to her previous routines, but instead used as a catalyst for rethinking what she had been doing.

A Contrast: Preserving Traditional Interpretations

There was a clear relationship between the teachers' emphasis on students' own thinking and the ways that they used the writing activities they developed during the project. Bush's and Moss's increasing emphasis on student thinking developed in concert with their new kinds of writing activities. Graves, on the other hand, resisted placing more emphasis on students' own ideas, and as a result the new writing activities did not play a very important role in his teaching. In his approach to writing about literature in ninth-grade English, he was using activities similar to those often promoted in the literature on writing instruction because of their value in helping students think through new ideas or experiences. In his class, however, the activities were redefined to fit more comfortably with his own teaching agenda. As Graves began to incorporate various process-oriented writing activities, he used them to reinforce rather than to change his conception of what counts as learning in English.

We can take as an example his lead-up to the final paper on *Romeo and Juliet*. In the formal paper, discussed in the previous chapter, he wanted his pupils to write about the alternatives Juliet has at the end of the play and her motivation for choosing to die. In the collaborative planning sessions, he decided that pupils might benefit from a series of short, unstructured writings in preparation for the final paper. The episode is an interesting illustration of the collaborative process at work, as he reinterpreted and assimilated new activities into his teaching.

During the planning session, Graves discussed several writing topics he had been considering as part of the unit, finally settling on character motivation. A three-part sequence of activities emerged from this session, as the research assistant working with him summarized the plan:

> *Writing #1:* Freewriting in which students describe a conflict, picking a difficult choice they had to make between several options and answering the following questions: "Why did you do what you did, and do you think it had anything to do with your training, your character, etc.?"
>
> *Writing #2:* A second freewriting encouraging students to begin to think about motivation — the hidden forces that affect characters' responses to conflict. In this piece, students could be asked to provide a brief description of some action of a character in the play and discuss what they think his or her motive for it was. (This was intended to address Graves's concern for the students' need to be able to decode the language of the play.)
>
> *Writing #3:* A final paper in which students are to discuss the motives that figure into Romeo's or Juliet's response to their conflicts — Romeo has to choose among his love, his family, and his honor; Juliet has to choose between marrying Paris and being faithful to Romeo.

From one point of view, this series of writings represented a natural extension of the process of writing a formal paper. The three papers would build upon one another and would help the students think through the issue of character motivation before dealing with it in a more formal way. Graves's initial rationale for this series of writings seemed to be: "I think a failure of my teaching, my writing assignments anyway, is that they tend to be sort of one-shot things, and the kids aren't normally primed — so [these are] good."

Personal experience and literary text, however, were two different things in his teaching, and by the time he introduced these assignments, they had been transformed to fit better into his classroom. The first freewriting exercise was introduced five days after the planning session. ("Freewriting" here was his term for any impromptu writing in which organization and content were not specified in advance.) The class followed the typical pattern, with three different activities during the period. The first twenty-six minutes were devoted to diagramming sentences, followed by seven minutes during which Graves read aloud from the play (part of his ongoing attempt to help students deal with the difficult language and give them a "feel" for the play). Thirty-three minutes into the class, he began the last activity for the day. He told the students to take out blank sheets of paper and reminded them to put their names at the top. He then said, "Now you're going to do some personal writing." He let them know that he would be collecting it at the end of the period and that he would read the papers but not grade them as he normally did.

He began the directions by saying,

> All right, what I want you to do is to think of a situation in which you had to make a decision that was difficult. Perhaps you were pulled in two different directions. Something you wanted, wanted to do, wanted to say that was difficult for you. I want you to write about that. I want you to say what you finally decided to do and why you decided, why you made the decision you did. What entered into your decision. It may take you a minute or two or three or four to think what to say, to write about. Think of some personal decision that you had to make where perhaps there were alternatives. [unclear] I'll write this on the board. You can be thinking while I'm writing.

Some students immediately began to write; others watched while he put the directions on the board. He wrote: "Write about making a decision, perhaps a difficult decision in the circumstances. What did you finally decide to do? What factors influenced your decision?" To this point the directions had taken three minutes.

Once the directions were on the board, most students went quietly to work. Six minutes into the freewriting, Lynn had filled roughly one-third of a page. Sandy had filled two-thirds of a page. One minute later, Suzanne turned her paper over and began filling the back side. Throughout this entire time, the classroom was very quiet.

After eight minutes, some of the students finished and some chatter began in the room. Others were still writing when Graves told them to turn in their freewritings along with the other work due that day. The last few minutes of class were filled with students' chatter and the teacher's individual conferences about tardies and past homework. After the class, Graves admitted that he had wondered whether the students would be able to write when given an immediate prompt like the one he had given in class. Having watched their efforts, he was amazed and pleased that students seemed to write quickly and at length.

During a prep period, he read through the students' responses and on several occasions responded aloud to what a student had written (for example, one student had had to put his dog to sleep). Graves said he was moved by their honesty and the emotion they could express on paper.

From what he reported as he read through these papers, the students did not elaborate on what influenced their choices. Graves, however, was concerned about the amount of time he would be able to spend with freewriting in the class. Rather than continuing work on this assignment or even picking up with the sequence discussed in the original planning session, he returned the papers the next day and moved along with discussion of the play. From his point of view, the assignment had served the purpose of motivating student interest.

At the end of the study of *Romeo and Juliet*, Graves introduced the formal essay on character motivation without referring to the earlier freewriting. (The discussion on Juliet's decision, used to introduce the formal essay, is described in detail in chapter 4.) Following his lead, the students approached the formal essay without reference to the earlier work. Sandy, who had been very involved in the freewriting, noticed a connection with the essay only afterwards under the influence of our prompting:

> Well, yeah, it . . . the first freewrite did seem like it was related to the play 'cause I wrote about my family. Oh God, I never thought that but yeah, it does relate really well except it's not a quarrel between two different families; it's a quarrel in a family.

When we asked Stan, the second case-study student, a similar question, he did not even remember writing about a personal decision.

In discussing this and similar sequences that took place during our work with Graves, he said he liked the idea of having pupils do a series of preliminary writings rather than typical one-shot writing assignments. He also said he found that the pupils were engaged in the writing process, as indicated by the "genuine voice" that came through the writing. The writing itself reflected this difference in engagement: 66 percent of the essays in response to the impromptu, personal writing assignment assumed a teacher-learner dialogue; 100 percent of the final papers were addressed to the teacher-as-examiner. Despite these observations, however, he admitted that he did not see the series of writings as a continuum, a position reflected in his teaching in a lack of explicitly articulated connections between the freewriting and the final assignment.

Graves's definition of student success was conditioned by his belief that meaning resides in the text. The path to knowledge, in his view, begins in the text, not in the knowledge his students bring to it. For him, their prior knowledge contributes to interest in, but not under-standing of, the texts. Given these beliefs, he found the freewriting a useful way to stimulate student interest, but not a way to develop the meaning of the text. Because their writing did not lead the students into the text, it was unnecessary for him to make explicit the connection between the text and the freewriting, since he was not interested in having the students build a coherent theory out of personal experience. Finally, if time became a problem, the freewriting could be dropped from the curriculum altogether without risking the students' potential understanding of the text.

In the course of our work with Graves, he never altered these fundamental constructs of what counts as learning. And, in turn, he never altered the nature of students' engagement with learning in his classes.

The Link between Changes in Evaluation and Changes in Teaching

Teachers' systems of evaluation were tightly tied to the kinds of changes they made as a result of their collaboration with us. In each of the classrooms where the project led to changes in the nature of learning, the teachers also changed the kinds of performance they valued and rewarded. In each case, these changes involved developing ways to examine students' own interpretations and their ability to muster relevant and coherent evidence for their beliefs. At the same time, the classrooms in which the teachers found ways to assimilate the new activities most fully to their previous methods of evaluation were those showing the greatest change in classroom activities without a change in the nature of learning.

Jane Martin is a good example that shows how new ways of evaluating student progress were closely linked with other changes in teaching and learning. As we have seen in chapter 3, during her first year on the project, her central concern was to protect her students from failure. To do this, she determined the important content to be learned, structured her lessons around that content, and expected students' responses to follow the pattern she had prepared. Even in discussion activities, her focus was on what she wanted to hear, rather than on what her students knew or were thinking.

In our early meetings with Martin, she had begun to talk about using writing to help her students explore in their own words the concepts they were studying, leading to a richer understanding of the information they were writing about. Despite this openness, her rules of classroom life were clear: it was the teacher's duty to impart knowledge, to structure the form and content of the lesson, and to evaluate student learning based upon the knowledge imparted. Given this framework, only during the middle of the second year of her participation in the project did Martin begin to find the words even to talk about the differences between her assumptions about teaching and her goals for student learning. Her ambivalence was evident. She admitted having an uncomfortable time reading her students' logs without correcting errors because, she said, "I thought, gee, I wonder if they know what's wrong here." She explained,

> What happens is we teachers start an assignment with a form in our mind and we know exactly what we want and we adapt things according to that form. Pushing the kids into it. You'll even find kids using words that you consider inappropriate and you have to pull back, you have to let them get the point for themselves. It's a very tough thing to let the kids go. I think the reason I do it [control so much of the student thinking] is I know where I want to go, and it's very hard for me to give that up. The kids want you to structure it because the kids are grade conscious and they know if I have some idea of what an "A" is that I'd better let them know so they can meet it. And the school system is structured. The textbook, the district competency test, the district objectives, all force me in a certain line of "This is where I have to be going." . . . Having the right answer makes teaching easier 'cause I know what I'm looking for. Not having the right answers makes it more chancy.

Martin struggled with this issue of evaluation and control throughout the two years she collaborated with us. Underlying it was her continued sense that not only did a certain body of knowledge have to be learned during each of her social studies units, but also that students needed to be able to recite their understanding in particular ways. These responses were her evidence that the students had learned the necessary information and that she had been a successful teacher. Support (or control) was her way of assuring the kind of successful recitation she considered so important.

Martin's approaches began to change only as she found new ways to handle the problem of evaluation. One of her successes during the second year came in a unit on Africa. In the unit she began to focus on more complex social studies skills, such as students' ability to draw inferences about the countries from the information they had collected: "If I say something like 'These people farm,' then how can I draw an inference like 'I would not expect most people to drive a car' or 'I wouldn't expect many people to live in big cities'?" She found it more difficult to ensure that her students would be successful at activities stressing such goals; her response was to provide even more structure for their work, confining her evaluation within that structure. Thus a letter-writing assignment about Africa told the students where to look for information and specifically warned them to "make inferences about what one will see":

> You have just looked at a variety of information about Africa. Pretend you learned all these things not from maps, but on a trip there. Now write a letter to a friend describing what he or she can expect to see in Africa. Include as much information as you can. See if you can take the information from the charts and make inferences about what one will see. For example, the low literacy rate might mean that signs are probably pictures rather than written. See how informative you can be.

Students wrote rough drafts in class, and Martin responded to the drafts with suggestions for improvement before the final drafts were completed in class. In talking about the assignment, she commented on the structure she expected and how she would evaluate papers within that structure:

> I want [the papers] to be limited to [discussions of] two or three categories. One category in a paragraph. For example, literacy is a category; health is a category. Say what they expect to find based on a category.... I'm going to evaluate these, probably, since I'm trying to teach [making] inferences and being logical, probably on the basis of how logical they are. Do they make sense or are they off the wall kind of thing.

Martin's criteria for evaluation, which she did not share with the class, suggested that she had a good idea of the content and form she was looking for.

Keith, one of the case-study students, had difficulty with the assignment until he got help from the teacher:

> At first what I thought she was looking for was just what you would write to somebody. Like I started out writing like that and she told me that I had to put a lot more there, like more facts,

so I had to change the way I was doing it. . . . So I just put a bunch more facts. She explained to me how to relate them to what I was writing about.

Martin was pleased with the results: "They did a lovely job. Their problem is not in making the inferences, it's in connecting the specific data. They talk too generally." Her sense of what would demonstrate learning influenced the assignment she gave, the instructional supports she provided along the way, and the evaluation criteria she used.

As her evaluation criteria changed, Martin began a transition to a different kind of teaching — a transition not completed until the second year of her participation in the project. When we first met Martin, her writing assignments were generally fill-in-the-blank exercises. This assignment on Africa, like many of her writing assignments during the second year, asked instead for a lengthy response and offered the students more room to add their own ideas. As she became more enthusiastic about such writing, she began to accept student interpretations of their new learning as evidence of student success rather than grade solely on the basis of accuracy in replicating what had been presented in the textbook or in class. She was aware of the changes in her approach and wanted them to become a more routine part of her instructional style. Yet the lesson on Africa reminds us how difficult a change this can be, even for a teacher as committed to change as Jane Martin.

Conclusions

Our look at teachers and classrooms in the process of assimilating a variety of writing activities leads us to several conclusions about the role of writing in academic classrooms. Across time, all of the teachers moved toward a new conceptualization of writing as a tool for learning *some* of the time — none of them incorporated new approaches to writing and learning *all* of the time. The extent to which they made such changes was governed by several factors, all related to their ideas of their roles as teachers and the students' roles as learners: what it means to teach, what it means to learn, and what should count as evidence of successful teaching and learning.

An overview of the seven teachers in the study and the changes that occurred during the course of their participation is provided in table 7. The central concerns that governed the classrooms (elaborated in chapter 3) remained constant throughout the study for all of the teachers, reflecting their deep-seated beliefs about how their classrooms

Table 7

The Teachers' Constructs of Teaching and Learning

	Central Concern	Role of Teacher	Evidence of Learning	Change in	
				Activities	Learning
Martin					
Initial	Protect students from error	Provide information	Accuracy		
Final		Provide information, elicit thinking	Accuracy, interpretation	Yes	Yes
Bardolini					
Initial	Provide information	Provide information	Accuracy		
Final		Provide information	Accuracy	Yes	No
Moss					
Initial	Foster content inquiry	Provide information	Accuracy		
Final		Elicit thinking	Accuracy, interpretation	Yes	Yes
Bush					
Initial	Foster content inquiry	Provide information, elicit thinking	Accuracy		
Final		Elicit thinking	Accuracy, interpretation	Yes	Yes
Royer					
Initial	Complete established routines	Provide activities	Participation		
Final		Provide activities	Participation	No	No
Watson					
Initial	Help students organize	Provide activities	Complete activities		
Final		Provide activities	Complete activities	Yes	No
Graves					
Initial	Understand traditional forms	Provide information, activities	Accuracy		
Final		Provide information, activities	Accuracy	Yes	No

should function. These beliefs were clarified and articulated in the course of the project but did not change.

At the same time, many of the activities that the teachers developed in the course of the project represented at least implicitly a change in the teachers' understanding of their own roles. In addition to worksheets with right answers, they developed essay tasks that allowed a variety of responses; in addition to quizzes to be graded, they introduced freewriting activities that were not always read by the teacher. For three of the seven teachers (Martin, Moss, and Bush), the cumulative effect of such changes was to alter their own characterizations of their roles as teachers. All three had begun the study convinced that a major part of their roles as teachers was to provide information. At the end, all three had redefined their roles to place more emphasis on the need for students to interpret and reinterpret what they were learning for themselves, with the teacher serving as helper and guide. In redefining their roles, they also developed a new perception of what could count as learning in their classrooms, placing more emphasis on students' interpretations (and the evidence for such interpretations) instead of responding solely to the accuracy of the evidence itself.

We have also seen that it is relatively easy to introduce new writing activities into most classrooms, as long as these activities fulfill important pedagogical functions. Teachers will reinterpret such activities in the process of assimilating them, to ensure that they function smoothly within the constraints and expectations governing their teaching. At the same time, however, process-oriented approaches to writing may contain the seeds of a more fundamental transformation in the nature of teaching and learning. In some classrooms, at least, the introduction of these activities changed the role of the teacher and the role of the student, leading to more emphasis on students' own interpretations and on their engagement in the process of learning.

For those who wish to reform education through the introduction of new curricula, the results suggest a different message. We are unlikely to make fundamental changes in instruction simply by changing curricula and activities without attention to the purposes the activities serve for the teacher as well as for the student. It may be much more important to give teachers new frameworks for understanding what to count as learning than it is to give them new activities or curricula. Experienced teachers in particular already have a large repertoire of activities that they can reorchestrate effectively as their own instructional goals change. For them, it is the criteria for judging students' learning that will shape how they implement new approaches. Learning activities are driven by their purposes in the classroom environment, and how activities are evaluated is one of the clearest expressions of those purposes.

Our examination of teachers in transition was particularly important in our evolving theory of instruction. Thus far, however, we have focused primarily on the teachers, the nature and uses of the activities they introduced, and their students' responses to those activities. To round out our understanding of the uses of writing in academic learning it is also necessary for us to understand writing as it is experienced by the students — how particular writing activities affect their thinking and learning. Our studies of learning addressed these issues and will be discussed in chapters 6 through 8.

III Studies of Learning

6 Learning from Writing: An Initial Approach

In our discussion so far, we have assumed a typical English teacher stance and have taken it for granted that writing can and should play an important role in instruction in various academic subject areas. The changes that this role implies are far reaching, however. No matter how much we may believe in the power of writing to foster learning, the case for such widespread change needs to be made very carefully.

To make that case, the next three chapters briefly review previous research as well as present our own findings. As will become clear, the previous work is far from conclusive, while our own studies highlight the complexities as well as the benefits of the role of writing in learning.

In recent years there has been an increased focus on the teaching of writing in subject classrooms; "writing to learn" and teaching "writing across the curriculum" have become favored slogans in the 1980s (see Langer, 1984a, 1986b). Yet this focus has been based more on practical wisdom than on research evidence. In fact, at the present time there is little research to support the assumption that writing will bring about a generalized benefit to learning; the previous work is far from conclusive. While common sense, personal experience, and educational lore all suggest that writing is an activity that can lead to extensive rethinking, revising, and reformulating of what one knows, few studies have been undertaken to learn *when* people learn from writing, *what* kinds of learning result from engagement in different writing experiences, or *how* writing can be used to help students understand and remember the material they read.

Studies of Learning from Writing

The best evidence about the effects of writing on learning would come from studies that examine it directly. Does writing about a new topic help writers understand the new material? Unfortunately, no research tradition has addressed this question. The closest we can come is to look at the long series of studies on the effects of adjunct questioning and similar activities, which have usually come from research in reading comprehension or study skills (for comprehensive reviews, see Applebee, 1984; Anderson and Biddle, 1975; Hamilton, 1985; Reder, 1980). Although examining only the simplest forms of writing activities, such studies (for example, Rothkopf, 1966, 1972) provide useful information about the effects of manipulating ideas (from text or memory) in the process of learning new material. The general conclusion that emerges from these studies is that any manipulation or elaboration of material being studied tends to improve later recall, but the type of improvement is very closely tied to the type of manipulation.

Studies of learning from text have examined several ways of responding to study activities requiring written responses that vary in length and format. Summarizing across studies, Anderson and Biddle (1975) found that studies requiring short-answer responses produced greater gains (in comparison with read-only control groups) than did studies requiring only multiple choice responses. Similarly, studies that have compared written with mental responses have generally found that the written responses led to better post-test performance (for example, Michael and Maccoby, 1961).

One way of interpreting these findings on response modes is related to the amount of elaboration or manipulation they require from the reader. Written responses require more active participation than non-written responses, and short-answer questions require more than multiple-choice items. Such an interpretation is consistent with the results of other studies that have looked directly at the effects of varying degrees of manipulation, elaboration, or "levels of processing" (Craik and Lockhart, 1972) on comprehension or recall (Barnett, Di Vesta, and Rogozinski, 1981; Di Vesta, Schultz, and Dangel, 1973; Frase, 1970, 1972; Schallert, 1976; Schwartz, 1980; Watts and Anderson, 1971). These studies assume that the more intermediate steps required to answer a question, the greater the depth of processing involved. In general, studies in this tradition have found that activities requiring greater depth of processing have stronger effects on comprehension and recall, although these effects may be attenuated if the task leads to selective focusing of attention on some parts of a passage to the exclusion of others.

A few studies have looked at the effects of note-taking, which requires more extensive writing than the other forms of study activities that have been examined. Early studies suggested that note-taking was more effective than read-only or listen-only conditions, though results were dependent on the strategies adopted and on whether the notes were available for later review (Di Vesta and Gray, 1972; Fisher and Harris, 1973; Schultz and Di Vesta, 1972).

In a later study, Bretzing and Kulhavy (1979) used four levels of note-taking to examine a depth-of-processing hypothesis. Their results suggest that note-taking is better than no note-taking and that the nature of the note-taking activity, not simply the additional time, is the critical feature. Bretzing and Kulhavy (1981) replicated this finding and found further that particular idea units were more likely to be recalled if they had been included rather than omitted in an individual's notes.

Glover et al. (1981) compared recall scores after five study tasks that varied in the extent of interaction with readers' previous knowledge. In general, they found the strongest effects for tasks that required readers to draw more extensively on their previous knowledge; paraphrase tasks led to better recall of passage information, while tasks that required the reader to make logical extensions led to higher rates of consistent intrusions. Glover et al. interpret such intrusions as evidence of the forming of "new" knowledge through the interaction of text information with what the readers already knew.

A few studies have examined more directly the effects of writing on learning. Newell (1984) examined the effects of note-taking, short-answer study questions, and analytic essay writing on passage recall, organization of passage-relevant knowledge, and ability to apply concepts in a new context. Using Langer's (1984b, 1984c) measure of organization of passage-relevant knowledge, he found significant differences favoring essay writing but not on the other measures. Essay writers also took more time to complete the study task, leaving it unclear whether the effects that he found were due to the nature of the task itself or were simply an artifact of taking more time to complete it.

Attempting to bridge the usual gap between process and product studies, Newell also used an adaptation of Flower's and Hayes's (1980b) think-aloud procedures to examine what the students were doing in the various tasks. He argued that differing patterns in think-aloud protocols may reveal the underlying causes of the differing patterns of learning in the experimental conditions. Newell's data show very different patterns in composing processes in the three conditions, raising the possiblity of eventually being able to relate specific features of a writer's behavior, such as the amount of planning or questioning, to specific types of learning effects.

Scardamalia and Bereiter (1985) have also examined the relationship between writing and thinking about a particular topic. They posit that when writing contributes to thought, it does so because of a dialectic set up between two problem spaces, one defined by the rhetorical problems of presenting a text, the other defined by the writer's topic knowledge and understanding. The data they report indicate that various kinds of procedural facilitation can be designed to enhance the underlying dialectic, leading to measurable changes in either the writing process or the writing product. These changes are inferred to reflect a more effective dialectic process, and in turn to reflect more thinking about the topic. These studies, however, provide evidence that the writing process has changed, but not that writers emerge with a better understanding of the topics they were writing about.

This brief overview of previous work suggests that we have yet to develop an adequate research base for the argument that writing activities can make a significant contribution to learning in general or to the development of higher level reasoning skills. Few studies have directly addressed these questions, and the related literature suggests that, to the extent that writing is related to learning, the relationships will be complex rather than straightforward.

Concerns such as these led us to focus directly on the ways that different kinds of writing-after-reading activities make a difference in students' thinking about and learning of their course material. In the following section, we report our first step in examining this issue, using a small sample of students and tasks; in chapters 7 and 8, we extend the approach to a larger sample and more complex comparisons.

The Initial Study

Early in the project's first year, we asked six high school juniors to participate in a study of the ways they approached writing about text and the effects that writing might have on learning what they read. All were living in an upper middle-class suburban community in the San Francisco Bay area and were average to above average students. The findings of this first, small study illustrate some of the broader issues with which we were concerned. We examined how the students approached three common study tasks: completing short-answer study questions, taking notes, and writing essays. These activities were chosen because we found them to be used most frequently by the science and social studies teachers participating in the first year of classroom studies. Two of these tasks, note-taking and study questions, were used by the collaborating teachers primarily to review and consolidate new material. The third task, writing an analytic essay, was used to help students reformulate and extend their knowledge.

To provide common material for the students to read and study, two social studies passages (766 and 1,721 words in length) were chosen from an eleventh-grade American history textbook. One passage was about economic expansion after the Civil War, and the other was about the Great Depression. (See Appendix 2 for synopses of all reading passages and their characteristics.) Both came from high school social studies textbooks but were about topics the students had not yet studied. In particular, we were interested in examining how the students' engagement in the different writing activities affected their learning of the subject matter presented in the passages. We wanted to study both the reasoning processes they used when they engaged in each activity and the changes in their topic knowledge that might be apparent afterward.

Each student met with us individually for two sessions a week apart. At each session, the student read one passage and was then asked to study the information presented by either completing study questions, taking notes, or writing an essay:

1. Note-taking: The students were told to read and take notes as they usually do in studying for school.
2. Study questions: The twenty-five study questions were typical of those found in social studies textbooks and worksheets and required the students to fill in the correct response or to write a brief response of two or three sentences to a particular question.
3. Essay writing: The essay prompted analytic writing: for example, "Given what you learned from the passage, what do you feel were the two or three most important reasons for industrial growth in the late nineteenth and twentieth centuries? Explain the reasons for your choices."

Tasks and order were counterbalanced across students so that four students completed each task.

What They Wrote

The writing produced in response to these three tasks was, as expected, very different. The study questions led to the least amount of writing, though the total text that resulted, including the question stems provided by the study questions, was considerably longer. For example:

> What were the major manufacturing industries in the United
> States at the turn of the century?
>
>   meat packing   iron & steel   lumber   clothing   textiles
>
> What did profits on goods, bank loans, and foreign investments
> have in common?
>
>   all had to do with the growth because of money, capital

Although the students' notes involved somewhat more text, it was very fragmentary:

> 1. 1920's — prosperity, high wages, large profits, sustained dividends, increasing sales, invest (stock market)
>
> 2. not fortunate — Indians, Spanish speakers, blacks whose skills weren't needed

And the essays produced more extended, cohesive writing:

> In the United States, between the late 19th century and early 20th century, industrial growth rose to above the highest level of any (other) nation . and this made the United States the premier manufacturing nation in the world. A large influx. *imp. Technology and continuous government aid, and backing, gr helped to create the nation industrial growth, which in turn boosted the United States' gross national product.
>
> Great steps in technology were made in the period between. . . .

The responses to the tasks looked different, but were the thinking and learning also different? If so, how?

Thinking and Learning

So that we could examine the ideas and information the students focused on while engaged in the three study tasks, they were trained to think aloud as they completed each task, verbalizing all the thoughts that came into their heads (Flower and Hayes, 1980a, 1980b; Langer, 1986b, 1986c).

The students also completed a topic-specific knowledge measure before each read-and-study activity and again three days after the activity. The measure involved free association related to five concepts central to the meaning of each passage ("Jot down everything you think of when you see each word or phrase"). The responses were scored for extent of topic-specific knowledge, using a system developed by Langer (1980, 1981, 1982, 1984b, 1984c). The scores provided an index of learning (measured by change in topic-specific knowledge) in response to the three tasks. (See chapter 7 for a fuller discussion of this measure and how it is scored.)

The students' think-aloud protocols and the measures of passage-specific knowledge provide some interesting insights into the kinds of learning and thinking prompted by each of the three study tasks.

The Kinds of Thinking Each Task Fostered

Like the writing that resulted, the think-aloud protocols for the three tasks looked very different.

Study questions. In answering the study questions, the students tended to (1) read the question, (2) restate the question, (3) occasionally scan their memory of the passage, (4) refer to the passage for answers, and (5) write the answer they had arrived at. In general, they did not review the question, nor did they revise their answers at a later time. Thus, throughout each of the twenty-five questions in the activity, the students' major attention was on restating the questions and locating specific information in the passage. When the protocol comments were segmented into communication units (each expressing a new thought or idea, as in the examples below), more than 85 percent of the communication units represented time when the students were searching the text, as opposed to writing or thinking about their ideas. The students paid little attention to what they thought they knew or had learned.

These patterns are evident in the following transcript excerpts:

> (1) What were the major manufacturing industries in the United States at the turn of the century?/ (2) Uhm, looking down the page,/ (3) factors of growth./ (4) No, it's under/ (5) I'm reading over/ (6) I don't see any/. . . . (11) they're looking for specific factors/ (12) uhhhh, ok, I found it at the bottom of the page/ (13) In 1900, for example, the main manufacturing industries were meat packing. . . .

Note-taking. Of all three tasks, note-taking focused most attention on the content of the passage. A third of the protocol comments occurred when the students were reading the text; the rest occurred when they were writing what they had found in the text or thinking about the specific content to include in their notes. However, they did think about the specific ideas in the passage as they considered what was being said and whether to include it in their notes. They spent little time considering how the ideas related to each other or to other things they knew. While engaged in the note-taking activity, the students tended to read the passage in small segments and to use the temporal structure of the passage to structure their notes. They did not stop to integrate the information into larger units that might have then been used to structure their notes. Instead, they tended to use the text's paragraphs as their organizational frame. These patterns are evident in the following transcript excerpts:

> (19) ok, so we're into part 2, a new section/ (20) uh, and this is talking about the not so fortunate people in the 20s/ (21) and uh, I'm going through to find the key words/ (22) and, ok, *not fortunate* to begin with/ (23) and then it lists some groups that

> weren't fortunate/ *Indians,* Spanish speaking Americans/ (24) I'll
> just say Spanish speakers. . . .

Essay writing. When engaged in essay writing, the students tended
to (1) read the text, (2) consider what they had read in terms of the
question they were to answer, (3) brainstorm for relevant ideas, and
(4) combine and recombine ideas as they constructed their own
interpretation and response. Thus during essay writing the students
gave more attention to generating, integrating, and evaluating the
ideas they were considering; less than 10 percent of their comments
occurred when referring back to the text. A typical excerpt from an
essay protocol looked like this:

> (98) So, I've got my opening paragraph right now/ (99) but I've
> got nothing to back it up, or anything like that/ (100) so I've got
> to go back and see what I've written/ (101) I want people to
> believe what I've said/ (102) So, I'm talking about, and the main
> question is what I personally feel were the most important reasons
> for industrial growth/ (103) and I've already said they were the
> technology and government aid, and backing/ (104) but I haven't
> said why/ (105) So, my second paragraph should probably
> start. . . .

Reasoning Operations

To more closely examine the differing approaches the students were
taking, we categorized each comment in the protocols according to
the type of thinking or reasoning it reflected. The seven categories
that were analyzed were drawn from a comprehensive system developed to permit examination of on-line thinking during reading and
writing tasks (see Langer, 1986b). These categories, described in detail
in Appendix 1, are summarized below:

Questioning. Uncertainties and incomplete ideas that the person has
at any point in developing the piece — related to the genre, content,
or text (no specified guess or expectation).
"What were the major manufacturing industries in the United States
at the turn of the century?"

Hypothesizing. Plans that the person makes about what will be
presented, based on the desired function of a particular piece of text.
"Maybe it's factors of growth."

Using schemata. The ideas being developed or explained, based on
the genre, content, or text.
"Not fortunate, to begin with."

Evaluating schemata. Evaluations and judgments made about the
ideas.

Table 8

Communication Units in Think-Aloud Protocols

	Study Questions	Note-taking	Essay Writing
No. of communication units	523	556	1,033
Percent writing	52.4	82.0	76.8
Percent reading	47.6	18.0	23.2
No. of protocols	4	4	4

"That's not right."

Making metacomments. Comments about the person's use or nonuse of particular content or textual information.

"I found it at the bottom of the page."

Citing evidence. The information the writer presents, the explanations the writer provides, or the evidence the writer develops to answer a question or carry out a hypothesis.

". . . cause it's shorter."

Validating. Information, implied or direct, that the plan was fulfilled or a decision made.

"That's what it was. Well, that's what they're like."

Each communication unit was identified as falling into one of the reasoning categories; we also noted whether that comment occurred when the student was reading (referring back to the text) or writing and thinking about new ideas.

First, let us look at the number of ideas the students reported, as reflected in the total number of communication units in each think-aloud. Almost twice as many ideas were thought about and reported for the essays as for the note-taking or study-question activities (see table 8). The students' comments focused proportionately more on writing for the essays and on reading for the study questions. In completing the study questions, the students were forced back to the text to locate their answers. Even so, the writing that these tasks required led to more comments about writing than about reading or rereading the text.

Specific Reasoning Activities Prompted by the Study Tasks

As the specific types of reasoning activities are looked at more closely, clear differences emerge from one task to another; the relevant data

Table 9

Reasoning Operations during Three Types of Writing Activities

	Percentage of Communication Units		
	Study Questions	Note-taking	Essay Writing
Questioning	24.3	0.2	7.5
Hypothesizing	9.0	11.6	19.9
Using schemata	47.2	66.2	44.3
Schemata evaluated	4.8	5.2	6.2
Making metacomments	11.6	9.0	12.2
Evidence and validation	2.1	6.6	7.5
Total	100.0	100.0	100.0
No. of communication units	523	556	1,033

are summarized across students in table 9. *Questioning* (a relatively open-ended search for an answer) took place more frequently in the study-question activity than in any of the others, reflecting the students' shifting focus as they moved from one question to the next on the worksheet. *Hypothesizing* (requiring a firm prediction about the topic under study) occurred most frequently in essay writing, when the students were thinking about what to write and whether it made sense. *Using schemata* (comments about the content itself) occurred in the greatest proportion during note-taking, when the specific ideas were either taken directly from the text or were restated in the student's own words. *Evaluating schemata* (showing evidence of active evaluation of information or ideas), *making metacomments* (when the students commented directly on their attempts to get at meaning), *citing evidence,* and *validating* previous interpretations all occurred most frequently when the students were writing essays.

Overall, the greatest variety of reasoning operations occurred during essay writing, suggesting that this type of activity provided time for students to think most flexibly as they developed their ideas. The smallest range of reasoning operations occurred during the study-question activity. Although the students did focus on passage content, their attention was generally limited to restatements either of the questions themselves or of the particular content unit that answered each question. Somewhat more variety in reasoning operations occurred during note-taking, but this too was text based, with only limited attention to the global sense of the passage.

Learning

If there were a difference in the kinds of thinking and reasoning that each activity invoked, we would also expect to find differences in the knowledge the students gained from engaging in the three activities. The analysis of topic knowledge was designed to help us look for these differences. Topic knowledge was measured before each read-and-study activity and again three days later. The measure used looks at both the amount of knowledge each student had about the key concepts in the passage and at the extent of organization the student had imposed upon what he or she knew.

For these students, topic knowledge increased most for essay writing, next for note-taking, and least for the study questions. The biggest difference, however, was between essay writing and the other two activities. (If we rank the twelve sets of gain scores so that 1 represents the most gain and 12 the least, the average rank was 5.1 for essay writing, 6.8 for note-taking, and 7.6 for study questions.) This finding suggests that the extended writing activity presented the students with the opportunity not only to think about the items of information in the passages they had read, but also to integrate the information into the more highly organized units of knowledge that were reflected in the topic-knowledge measure.

Discussion

Even from these initial explorations, it is apparent that different study activities involved students in very different patterns of thinking and also led to different kinds of learning: (1) When completing the short-answer study questions, the students focused on specific ideas that the textbook writer had chosen. They thought about these ideas in an item-by-item fashion, with no integration of content across questions. (2) When taking notes, the students focused on larger concepts than when they completed short-answer study questions; they integrated ideas across sentence boundaries. However, while this led to concern with larger chunks of meaning, the ideas were treated relatively superficially. The students listed the information in a linear fashion in much the same way that it was presented in the text and did not reorganize it in their own ways. (3) When writing essays, the students seemed to step back from the text after reading — they reconceptualized the content in ways that cut across the specific information presented, focusing on larger issues or topics. In doing so, they integrated information and engaged in more complex thought. Of all three activities, when writing essays the students seemed least bound by the immediate content, focusing instead on manipulating and reorganizing the new material. When doing the study questions, on the other hand, the students seemed to focus on many more individual content units but in a more cursory manner.

The results from this first study of student learning reinforced our initial expectations about the relationships between writing and learning and led us to undertake two larger scale studies examining the effects of various kinds of writing activities on learning. Results of these studies are presented in chapters 7 and 8.

7 Learning from Writing: Study Two

The differences that emerged in the initial case study led us to explore more systematically the effects that various classroom tasks have on learning from text. The second study examined a broader range of tasks and passages and tested the effects over a longer term (one month instead of a few days). We had two primary concerns: (1) to document the longer term effects of writing versus not writing (represented by a read-and-study task), and (2) to explore the effects of writing tasks that require reformulation of new information versus simpler ones that focus on review. For reformulation, we developed tasks requiring analytic writing; for review, we chose two typical approaches, note-taking and answering comprehension questions.

Participants

For this study, we obtained the cooperation of the English department of a local secondary school. A sample of 208 students was drawn from six ninth-grade and six eleventh-grade classes. The students represented the full spectrum of abilities at each grade level, except that classes for English as a second language and classes for the educationally mentally handicapped were excluded from the sample.

Passage Selection

Four passages were selected from high school social studies texts. Two of the passages ("economic expansion" and "the Great Depression") were those used in the exploratory study, and two additional passages were selected for the present study. One of these dealt with political and economic developments in Russia after World War II; the other discussed the influence of science on life in the twentieth century. Though drawn from longer units, all four passages were self-contained and able to stand alone. (See Appendix 2 for synopses of the four passages and their characteristics.)

Study Conditions

Four study tasks were designed for each passage: normal studying, note-taking, comprehension questions, and analytic writing.

Normal studying. Students in the normal studying condition were told simply, "Study the way you normally do to remember the information in the passage." This condition allowed us to examine how students would approach the task when allowed to choose their own methods.

Note-taking. Students in the note-taking condition were told, "Take notes to help you learn the information in the passage." This is a review activity that allows the students to concentrate on the material they consider most relevant.

Comprehension questions. For the comprehension-question condition, we designed a series of short-answer questions similar to those that students encounter in workbook study guides and teacher-made dittos. Review activities of this sort focus the students' attention on specific aspects of the passages. For each of the four passages, twenty questions were devised and divided equally among textually explicit and textually implicit questions. Sample items about "economic expansion" follow:

> Please answer the following questions as you would answer questions for a homework assignment.
> *Economic Expansion:*
>   What were the major manufacturing industries in the United States at the turn of the century?
>   What did profits on goods, bank loans, and foreign investments have in common?

Analytic writing. In the analytic-writing assignments, the students were asked to reformulate and extend the material from the passages as they developed evidence to support a particular interpretation or point of view. For "economic expansion," the students were asked to respond to the following question:

> Given what you learned from the passage, what do you feel were the two or three most important reasons for industrial growth in the late nineteenth and early twentieth centuries? Explain the reasons for your choices.

Measures

Three instruments were designed to examine what students had learned in the process of reading and studying the passages. These measures are described below.

Topic Knowledge

Langer's (1980, 1981, 1982, 1984b, 1984c) measure of passage-specific knowledge was used to measure students' knowledge of the topic and how it changed as a result of particular study activities. Students were asked to provide written free-association responses to five key concepts drawn from the top half of the content hierarchy in each passage (see Meyer, 1975, 1981). An unrelated concept (dog) was used as a practice item before the five words were presented. Practice exercises were given orally, and students were paced through the free-association task one concept at a time. Sufficient space was left between concepts so that the students could provide as many associations as possible.

The measure was scored to reflect a combination of the amount (breadth) and organization (depth) of passage-relevant information reflected in the free associations, using procedures developed by Langer (1980, 1984b, 1984c; Langer and Nicholich, 1981). For each concept word in the knowledge measure, each free association was scored as indicating (1) peripheral knowledge of the concept, (2) concrete understanding (such as examples, attributes, defining characteristics), or (3) abstract understanding (such as superordinate concepts, definitions). Ratings reflecting levels 2 and 3 were then summed across concepts and raters to derive a total score for each passage. Interrater reliability for the total score (estimated using the Spearman-Brown formula) was .875. The test-retest correlation was .712 after four weeks and an intervening treatment period.

The measure was administered three times: before the students had read the passage, immediately after reading it, and four weeks later. As a pretest, this measure reflects students' prior knowledge of the topics they read about; changes between the pretest and the post-test provide a measure of what the students learned as a result of the reading and study activities.

Passage Comprehension

A twenty-item multiple-choice test was constructed for each passage to measure overall comprehension. Eight items required a simple report of information from the passage, eight required the student to construct relationships among items of information in the passage, and four required drawing generalizations that extended beyond the passage. To ensure that items and distractors were functioning as intended, the items for each test were developed through a cycle of pilot testing that included interviews exploring the participants' reasons for their answers. The twenty items for each passage were randomly ordered and administered once, four weeks after the initial read-and-study tasks. The multiple-choice items were scored right or wrong and summed to give the total number correct (out of twenty) for each passage.

Application of New Information

The final measure was an extended essay that required students to orchestrate what they had learned in a coherent argument based on information from the original reading. Though requesting the same type of writing as the analytic-writing study condition, the format of the prompt and specific topic differed in each case. The essay was administered at the four-week post-test. For example, the instructions for "economic expansion" read:

> Write an essay based on what you learned from the reading on economic expansion. Use the title, "Causes and Effects of Industrial Growth at the Turn of the Century." Be certain to support the points you make.

The essays were ranked by two independent raters on the basis of overall coherence and the structure of the argument developed, rather than on the conventions of standard written English. The essays from the four passages were scored on a single scale from best to worst. Tables of the normal distribution were used to convert each rater's scores to a normally distributed scale ranging from 22 (best) to 1 (worst). Scores for the two raters were then summed to yield an essay-quality score with a sample mean of 23.2 and standard deviation of 7.5. Interrater reliability for the total score (estimated using the Spearman-Brown formula) was .94. This procedure, though obviously not feasible in larger scale assessments, provided much better discrimination among essays than would have been gained from more common 4-point or 6-point holistic or general impression rating scales.

Procedures

Separate but overlapping sets of three passages were used at each grade level (ninth and eleventh). The "Great Depression" was used only with eleventh graders; "twentieth-century science" only at grade nine. At each grade level, two classes were assigned at random to each passage. (Passages were assigned by class to simplify administration of passage-specific measures.) Study packets were assembled so that students within classes were randomly assigned to one of the four study conditions.

During the first day of the study, the students completed the passage-specific knowledge measure, followed by a packet containing (1) general directions to read the passage and then to complete the task that followed, (2) the reading passage, and (3) directions for the study task. Ten minutes before the end of class, the passages and study packets were collected and the passage-specific knowledge measure was re-administered. Students had seven minutes for each administration of the knowledge measure, and thirty-five minutes to read the passage and complete the study task. The study tasks thus functioned as post-reading activities, with the reading passage available while the study tasks were completed.

Exactly four weeks later, all classes completed the three measures of learning. The passage-specific knowledge measure was given first, followed by the essay test focusing on comprehension of relationships within the original passage. The multiple-choice comprehension tests were administered last so that the questions and answers would not provide students with additional information to draw upon in completing the other measures. Again, all measures were completed within a single class period, with seven minutes for the passage-specific knowledge measure, twenty minutes for the essay, and twenty minutes for the comprehension test. (At this session, students did not have any of the materials from the original study session available to them.)

Responses to the Study Tasks

The pretest measure of passage-specific knowledge provides a test of the initial comparability of the four groups. The relevant results, summarized in table 10, indicate that students in the four study conditions did differ somewhat in the extent of their initial passage-specific knowledge. The normal studying and the note-taking groups had somewhat higher initial knowledge of the topics discussed in the passages they read. Grade level differences were not significant because of the use of an additional, easier passage with the ninth graders and an additional, harder passage with the eleventh graders. (The eleventh graders had significantly greater passage-specific knowledge than did the ninth graders for the two passages given to both grade levels, F $(1;202) = 14.56, p < .001$.) Because of the initial differences in passage-specific knowledge, the analyses that follow use initial passage-specific knowledge as a covariate in order to provide a statistical adjustment for the initial group differences.

The amount that students wrote in response to each study task provides one indication of the amount of cognitive effort that they

Table 10

Characteristics of Student Performance on Selected Study Tasks

	Adjusted Means			
	Essay ($n = 53$)	Comprehension Questions ($n = 47$)	Note-taking ($n = 54$)	Normal Studying ($n = 54$)
Pretest passage knowledge				
Grade 9	11.4	10.7	11.9	13.2
Grade 11	12.8	10.2	16.3	13.1
	(Pooled within-cell $SD = 8.15$)			
Words written during task				
Grade 9	99.4	114.2	101.1	21.7
Grade 11	123.5	94.5	155.1	54.1
	(Pooled within-cell $SD = 52.99$)			

Analysis of Variance

Effects	Initial Passage Knowledge			Task Words		
	df	F	p	df	F	p
Task	3	2.62	.052	3	21.52	.001
Grade	1	2.41	.122	1	0.38	n.s.
Passage	3	31.15	.001	3	6.02	.001
Task × passage	9	1.47	.160	9	0.83	n.s.
Task × grade	3	0.30	n.s.	3	0.28	n.s.
Passage × grade	1	1.84	.176	1	3.94	.049
Task × passage × grade	3	0.71	n.s.	3	0.14	n.s.
Error	184			184		

put into each task. In turn, we would expect the amount of effort to be related to the amount of learning that resulted. These data are also summarized in table 10. As would be expected, the eleventh graders wrote more than the ninth graders, and the normal studying group wrote on average less than the groups that were specifically asked to write. At grade nine, the three types of writing tasks produced relatively similar amounts of writing, but at grade eleven they diverged somewhat, with comprehension questions producing the least writing and note-taking the most.

Table 11

Multiple-Choice Comprehension at Four Weeks

	Adjusted Means			
	Essay (*n* = 53)	Comprehension Questions (*n* = 47)	Note-taking (*n* = 54)	Normal Studying (*n* = 54)
Grade 9	9.0	9.0	9.2	8.7
Grade 11	9.6	10.8	10.4	10.6

(Pooled within-cell *SD* = 2.63)

Analysis of Variance[a]

Effects	*df*	*F*	*p*
Task			
Linear	1	0.41	n.s.
Deviations from linear	2	0.05	n.s.
Grade	1	8.78	.003
Passage	3	29.92	.001
Task × passage	9	1.19	n.s.
Task × grade	3	1.64	.181
Passage × grade	1	0.01	n.s.
Task × passage × grade	3	0.88	n.s.
Covariate	1	19.37	.001
Error	183		

[a] Task × passage × grade, covaried on pretest passage knowledge.

Effects of Study Tasks on Learning

To what extent did the different study conditions lead to different effects on learning? Results for the multiple-choice comprehension test are summarized in table 11. The effects of most interest, those involving tasks, reflect differences among the four study conditions. These effects are partitioned into linear and deviations from linear effects in order to reflect the ordering of the four tasks from the most focused (essay) to the least focused (normal studying). The results indicate that there were no differences among the four study tasks in their effects on the multiple-choice comprehension task given at the four-week post-test, though passage and grade level both had a significant effect on post-test performance.

Results for the passage-specific knowledge measure are summarized in table 12. They indicate that the essay-writing group scored consistently lower than groups in the other conditions, and the normal studying group did consistently better at both the immediate and four-week post-test. The magnitude of this difference was greatly reduced at four weeks, a trend that is reflected in the task (linear) × time interaction ($p < .113$). The scores at the immediate post-test suggest that the essay task focused students' attention on a narrower range of information in the passage, thus providing them with fewer specific associations for the passage knowledge measure and leading to lower passage-specific knowledge scores. In contrast, the normal studying and note-taking conditions may have led students to distribute their attention more evenly over information in the passage as a whole, providing a broader base of associations on which they could draw and thus higher passage-specific knowledge scores. On the other hand, groups that showed the greatest immediate gains also showed the greatest falling off between the immediate and four-week post-tests: the decline from immediate to four-week post-test averaged 3 percent for the essay-writing group, 6.8 percent for the comprehension-question group, 10.5 percent for note-taking, and 11.5 percent for normal studying. Thus the normal studying and note-taking conditions seem to have led to an initial greater breadth of knowledge, but this knowledge was not retained as well.

The third measure from the four-week post-test was the quality of the essay that required students to apply what they remembered from the passage in support of an argument or interpretation. For this measure, consistent task differences again appeared, but in the opposite direction from those that occurred for the passage knowledge measure: the essay and comprehension-question conditions were consistently superior to the normal studying and assigned note-taking groups (table 13). At grade nine, the essay-writing group performed better than the comprehension-question group, but at grade eleven the performance of the two groups was indistinguishable.

It is interesting that the essay scores showed task differences favoring the more focused writing conditions at four weeks even though the other measures did not. The essay task differed in three important ways from the other two outcome measures: it provided fewer cues to recall, required orchestration of relationships among the information that was remembered, and could be completed successfully using a narrower selection of information from the original passage. This finding suggests that the two study conditions requiring the most focused writing — the essay and comprehension-question study tasks —

Table 12

Passage-Specific Knowledge: Immediate and at Four Weeks

	Adjusted Means			
	Essay (*n* = 51)	Comprehension Questions (*n* = 45)	Assigned Notes (*n* = 53)	Normal Studying (*n* = 53)
Immediate post-test				
Grade 9	17.8	19.2	22.0	22.8
Grade 11	20.9	24.8	22.6	27.8
	(Pooled within-cell *SD* = 7.74)			
Four-week post-test				
Grade 9	18.3	18.1	20.1	20.9
Grade 11	19.2	22.9	19.8	23.9
	(Pooled within-cell *SD* = 8.09)			

Repeated Measures Analysis of Variance[a]

Effects	*df*	*F*	*p*
Between subjects			
Task	2	2.40	.070
Linear	1	6.47	.012
Deviations from linear	2	0.35	n.s.
Passage	3	5.24	.002
Grade	1	0.82	n.s.
Task × passage	9	0.66	n.s.
Task × grade	3	1.02	n.s.
Passage × grade	1	16.41	.001
Task × passage × grade	3	1.40	n.s.
Covariate	1	100.78	.001
Error	177		
Within subjects			
Time	1	10.92	.001
Task × time	3	0.99	n.s.
Linear	1	2.54	.113
Deviations from linear	2	0.21	n.s.
Passage × time	3	9.81	.001
Grade × time	1	2.88	.091
Task × passage × time	9	0.18	n.s.
Task × grade × time	3	0.31	n.s.
Passage × grade × time	1	2.47	.118
Task × passage × grade × time	3	0.45	n.s.
Error	178		

[a] Task × passage × grade × time, with pretest passage knowledge as a covariate.

Table 13

Essay Quality at Four Weeks

	Adjusted Means			
	Essay ($n = 46$)	Comprehension Questions ($n = 42$)	Note-taking ($n = 49$)	Normal Studying ($n = 48$)
Grade 9	23.5	21.6	20.6	20.8
Grade 11	27.2	27.6	23.3	24.0

(Pooled within-cell $SD = 6.87$)

Analysis of Variance[a]

Effects	df	F	p
Task			
Linear	1	4.26	.041
Deviations from linear	2	0.95	n.s.
Grade	1	1.33	n.s.
Passage	3	3.67	.014
Task × passage	9	1.29	n.s.
Task × grade	3	0.48	n.s.
Passage × grade	1	0.55	n.s.
Task × passage × grade	3	0.23	n.s.
Covariate	1	8.36	.004
Error	160		

[a] Task × passage × grade, covaried on pretest passage knowledge.

may have led to a deeper understanding of a narrower body of information than did the note-taking and normal studying tasks.

Effect of Amount Written on Post-test Performance

When we examined the number of words written during the study task, we hypothesized that the number would reflect the cognitive effort students put into their writing. That is, we would also expect that writing *more* would be related to better post-test performance, whatever particular writing task a student may have been assigned. To examine this hypothesis, we can look at the relationship between the amount written during the study task and post-test performance after accounting for all of the other factors and covariates in the model (passage, task, grade level, and pretest passage-specific knowledge).

Table 14 presents the relevant pooled within-cell correlations for each study condition separately and for all four groups pooled. In

Table 14

Relationships between Words Written during Study Task and Post-test Performance, Adjusted for Task, Grade, Passage, and Pretest Passage Knowledge

Measures	Adjusted Within-Cell Correlation with Words Written during Study (*df*)				
	Essay	Compre-hension Questions	Note-taking	Normal Studying	All
Essay quality	.451**	.290*	.014	.273*	.240***
	(39)	(35)	(42)	(41)	(160)
Passage knowledge					
Immediate	.301*	.259*	.158	.283*	.234***
	(44)	(40)	(47)	(46)	(180)
Four weeks	.415**	.525***	.082	.190	.292***
	(46)	(38)	(46)	(47)	(180)
Multiple-choice	.023	.314*	.038	−.104	.026
Comprehension	(46)	(40)	(47)	(47)	(183)

* $p < .05$
** $p < .01$
*** $p < .001$

general, performance on the multiple-choice comprehension test showed little relationship to the amount written for any of the groups except for the one that had answered similar questions during the study period. For the other measures, the amount written in response to either the essay task or the comprehension questions was positively and significantly related to post-test performance. Interestingly, for the passage knowledge measure these effects are stronger at four weeks than at the immediate post-test — a reflection perhaps of recency effects in initial responses to that measure. The consistent positive relationships for students in the essay-writing and comprehension-question study tasks indicate that, for these types of writing at least, the writing process itself may be directly related to the learning that results. For the other two conditions, note-taking and normal studying, the effects on learning may be associated with spending time with the material, whether or not much writing is involved. It is important to remember that the correlations have been corrected for pretest per-formance; they are not simply the result of good students doing better in everything including writing more.

Discussion

Results from this study are interesting but complicated. Rather than showing general effects, the results show that task differences favoring writing emerge only on the more complex and time consuming of the outcome measures, the essay requiring students to use what they had learned in order to mount an argument of their own. The other measures, which may have tapped a broader spectrum of remembered information, either show no differences or yield results favoring the normal studying and note-taking conditions.

The superior performance of the two focused writing groups on the four-week essay is encouraging, given our general hypotheses about the relationships between writing and reasoning. On the other hand, the effects are relatively small, and the differences among the various conditions are difficult to untangle. Results from the immediate post-test using the topic-knowledge measure suggest that the essay task may have focused students' attention on a narrower band of information, though by four weeks the advantage to the other conditions had been considerably reduced. The evidence from the within-cell correlation measures also suggests that there may be a relationship between what was written about and what was remembered, at least when students were completing focused writing tasks. At the least, writing more seemed to be related to how much was remembered later.

A third study, presented in chapter 8, was designed to pursue some of the questions raised by the one presented here. With more focused measures of outcomes, would clearer differences be discernable among various types of writing tasks? Could behavior during the study task, reflected here only in the number of words written during the treatment, be more directly traceable to post-test performance? If other types of focused writing were required, would they yield outcomes comparable to those for the essay-writing and comprehension-question conditions in the second study?

8 Learning from Writing: Study Three

For the third study in the series investigating the effects of writing on learning, we examined the relationship between what students did during the study task and what they remembered later. We were concerned with both the particular information focused on during the study task and the type of focus, as determined by the demands of various writing tasks. Also, we shifted our attention from the essay used as a criterion measure in the previous study to a measure of students' recall of particular content from the passages they had read. This allowed us to trace students' overt attention to particular items of content from the reading passages, first as they appeared in the material produced as part of the treatment condition, and later in measures of immediate and longer term recall.

We reduced the number of passages and students in order to examine each protocol in more detail and also reduced the time between the study task and the post-test in order to detect task differences that might not be evident a month after a single intervention. We assumed that such differences might be of practical importance under ordinary classroom conditions, in which writing tasks are often longer lasting, better motivated, and more cumulative than those contrived for the experimental situation. The tasks examined included a read-and-study condition (with no writing), two review-writing tasks (comprehension questions and summary writing), and one task requiring reformulation and extension of information in the passage (an analytic essay). The summary-writing task was added at this point in our studies because of its emerging importance in the parallel strand of classroom studies, discussed in chapters 3 through 6.

Thus this third study of writing and learning compared the kinds of behaviors and learning that result when students engage in four different kinds of tasks:

1. Read and study, but no writing
2. Comprehension questions (twenty short-answer questions)
3. Summary writing
4. Analytic writing

115

We were interested in seeing how the students approached each task in terms of the kinds and amount of material they manipulated (thought or wrote about) and what they recalled in both the short and the long term, that is, after one day and after five days.

Participants

The 112 students who participated in this study were ninth-grade and eleventh-grade students drawn from four of the six classes we studied in the project's second year. Mean student achievement levels were average on a variety of regularly administered, nationally normed achievement batteries.

Passages and Tasks

In developing the study tasks, we selected two passages from those used in the previous study: "postwar Russia" and "economic expansion." (Synopses of the passages and their characteristics appear in Appendix 2.) For each passage, we designed four different study tasks, each of which we expected would lead to a different kind of effort and engagement during the study period: read and study, comprehension questions, summary writing, and analytic writing.

Read and study. For the read-and-study condition, students were asked simply, "Study the reading passage. Do *not* do any writing." This instruction successfully inhibited the spontaneous note-taking that had occurred in the previous study.

Comprehension questions. The comprehension-question condition was identical to that in the second study. The twenty questions that were devised for each of the passages were divided equally among textually explicit and textually implicit questions.

Summary writing. The summary-writing task was designed to prompt review of the new material in an extended, cohesive text. Students received the following assignment: "In your own words, write a 200–250 word summary of the passage you just read."

Analytic writing. The analytic-writing assignments were designed to require the students to reformulate and extend the material from the reading passages as they developed evidence to support a particular interpretation or point of view. Topics were identical to those used in the second study.

Measures

Two outcome tasks were used, each yielding two or more measures; the tasks and scoring procedures are described below.

Topic Knowledge

Langer's (1980, 1981, 1984b, 1984c) measure of passage-specific knowledge was again used to measure the ways that the students' knowledge of the topic changed as a result of having engaged in the particular study activity. Three key concept words or phrases from the top half of the content hierarchy (see Meyer, 1975) were selected for each of the two passages. The six words were intermixed and administered as a single set of concepts. Students were asked to provide written free associations to each of the six concepts. Scoring of the measure reflected both the amount (breadth) and organization (depth) of passage-relevant information reflected in the free associations, following the procedures outlined in the previous chapter. Two scores were derived for each student, one for the target passage and one for the other passage in the study, which served as a control condition.

Recall Tasks

For the recall tasks, students were asked, "Please write down everything you can remember about the passage that you read." The recall protocols were scored for number of words, mean number of words per T-unit (Hunt, 1965), and preservation of the original gist of the passage. Ratings for gist were a holistic score reflecting the extent to which each recall showed an understanding of the overall gist or meaning of the original passage. Raters used a four-point scale, ranging from 1 (no reflection of the original gist) to 4 (very good preservation of original gist). Interrater agreement in an independent rating of a subset of thirty recalls was .87. (Though cast somewhat differently, the measure of gist is an overall measure of quality, parallel in its emphasis on coherent understanding to the holistic essay score in the previous study.)

In order to relate the information included in the recall tasks to the original passages, we first analyzed each passage for hierarchical content structure, using our adaptation of Meyer's (1975, 1981) prose analysis system (see Langer, 1986b). For this analysis, each passage was divided into sequentially numbered T-units, which were then analyzed in terms of their rhetorical relationships to other information in the passage. For example, content units appearing at level 2 of the content hierarchy are very central to the major theme of the passage, while those at levels 4 and 5 are explanations and elaborations of the higher level ideas. Two project team members analyzed each passage; differences were resolved by a third analyst. (The tree diagrams for each passage appear in Appendix 2.) The first passage, "postwar Russia," contained eighty-one content units; the second passage, "economic expansion," contained fifty content units.

The tree diagrams were used to examine students' responses during the study and recall tasks, content unit by content unit. A particular content unit was counted as "included" if any of the central ideas from the original T-unit appeared at any place during the study or recall task. Interrater agreement for the inclusion of individual T-units was .95 for two raters who separately scored a subsample of twenty recalls.

From these analyses, we defined *content units manipulated* as content units from the passage that also appeared at any point in the written material from the three study tasks that required writing: comprehension questions, summary writing, and analytic writing. *Content units recalled* were defined as any content units from the original passage included in the student's written recall. These were further subdivided to reflect level of the content unit in the original passage hierarchy and to reflect whether the content unit had been manipulated during the study task.

Procedures

During the class period when they regularly met with the project's participating teachers, the students were asked to complete the measure of passage-specific knowledge and then to read one of the two social studies passages, which were assigned randomly within each class. After reading the passages, the students engaged in one of the study conditions: rereading and studying, answering comprehension questions, summarizing, or writing a paper that asked them to defend a particular interpretation based on the text. The passages, which were prepared with instructions for the study conditions placed after the reading, were randomly distributed through the class. Students had the passages available while they completed the assigned study tasks. Eight additional students (four high and four low ability) engaged in think-aloud procedures to enable us to examine the reasoning and recall strategies that the students typically used in completing the different types of tasks. The passage-specific knowledge measure was repeated during class the following day (day two of the study).

Five days after the initial study task (on day six of the study), students completed the passage-specific knowledge measure for a third time, followed by the recall task. Passages and materials from the earlier study sessions were not available during either of the post-test sessions.

Background Characteristics

Before examining the effects of the various study conditions on subsequent performance, we need to consider students' initial knowledge of the content of the two passages and their behavior during the study tasks. The results for the pretest measure of passage-specific knowledge, summarized in table 15, indicate that students had similar amounts of background information about the two topics, but also that students showed some variation among study conditions in the extent of their knowledge ($p < .07$). Because of this, the analyses of learning outcomes that follow use pretest passage knowledge as a covariate to adjust statistically for any initial differences among the students in the four groups.

To understand the effects of the various tasks on student learning, we also need to examine the types of effort and engagement engendered by the tasks themselves. Three of the tasks (comprehension questions, summary writing, and analytic writing) asked for written responses. The general characteristics of these responses are also summarized in table 15.

In terms of number of words written during each of the treatment conditions, the students did the most writing when asked to summarize the passage and the least when asked to write analytically about what they had read. Because the comprehension questions used as a study condition could often be answered somewhat telegraphically, relying upon words in the question stem rather than repeating them, the word count may be somewhat misleading as a measure of the extent of engagement with particular content. If we examine instead the proportion of content units that were mentioned in the course of the study task, the picture looks somewhat different. Responses to the comprehension questions touched on a higher proportion of content units (26 percent) than did responses to either of the extended writing tasks. As in total number of words, analysis writing involved the smallest proportion of content from the original passage (15 percent).

From these data we might conclude that the comprehension questions led the students through the most thorough review of the material

Table 15

Background Measures: Pretest Passage Knowledge and
Characteristics of Performance during Study Tasks on Day One

		Means			
			Compre-hension		
	(Pooled SD)	Read and Study (n = 29)	Ques-tions (n = 29)	Summary Writing (n = 29)	Analytic Writing (n = 25)
Pretest passage knowledge					
Passage 1 concepts	(3.8)	2.1	4.4	2.6	4.1
Passage 2 concepts	(3.1)	3.0	3.7	2.7	4.4
Performance during study task					
Words	(56.5)	—	132.8	150.6	120.5
Words/T-unit	(2.8)	—	7.4	12.6	13.6
Content units included					
(%)	(8.6)	—	26.0	19.2	15.3

Analysis of Variance

		Effects							
		Task (Linear)		Task (Devia-tions)		Passage		Interaction	
Variable	df Error	F	p	F	p	F	p	F	p
Passage knowledge									
Passage 1	104	1.41	n.s.	2.70	.072	0.34	n.s.	0.42	n.s.
Passage 2	104	1.11	n.s.	1.65	.197	0.90	n.s.	1.21	n.s.
Performance during study task									
Words	63	0.53	n.s.	2.64	.109	7.09	.010	1.13	n.s.
Words/T-unit	63	54.95	.001	8.17	.006	1.02	n.s.	0.63	n.s.
Content units	61	14.46	.001	0.37	n.s.	4.40	.041	3.39	.041

they were studying and that the analytic-writing condition, in contrast,
led them to focus most narrowly on a subset of that information in
the process of reformulating and extending it. The analytic-writing
task also led to more complex syntax, as reflected in the measure of
words per T-unit. This finding is consistent with the hypothesis that
analytic writing leads to more complex interrelating of ideas in the
course of reformulating the material in order to develop and defend
a thesis or argument.

The students' think-aloud protocols also reflected differences among the study tasks. To complete the comprehension questions, Mark's think-aloud began like this:

> What were the major manufacturing industries in the U.S. at the turn of the century? Shoot. That's the biggest question. Okay, I thought they said it was meat-packing, and iron, and steel, textiles, and clothing. . . . Let me think. They said something else. Where is it? Umm, this, er, economic growth. Okay, *meat packing*. . . . [copies directly from text].

In general, the think-alouds indicated that the comprehension questions led the students to focus on the specific information in the passages they were reading. They searched the passage for the correct response, copied it once it was found, and never rethought that response or returned to change an answer. Although the questions forced them to think about specific items of content, they made little attempt to rework the material and no attempt to draw relationships across different questions.

In comparison, the students who participated in the summary task relied on the text for temporal order instead of the "right" answer. They ordered their summaries to reflect the paragraph-by-paragraph development of the original passage. In doing so, they also tended to review the relationships among the ideas that were presented in the original passage, recasting those ideas somewhat more in their own language. The summary students reviewed less content than did the comprehension-question group (since they were not prompted to search for responses to the twenty questions), but they did tend to search for more relationships among the ideas they dealt with.

The following excerpt from Doug's think-aloud for the summary task reflects the focus on temporal ordering and interrelating of ideas at least from adjacent passage segments:

> Okay, some of the main things they were making were. . . . Hm. . . "24 billion dollars, rapid growth. . . ." Okay, *the things which were in most demand after the Civil War were what was produced. Things like shoes, meat, textiles,* um, *etc.* Um, let's see what the other things were. Something relates back to that. 79 percent increase, coal, oil. *Industry had increased in the U.S. by 79 percent.* . . . That's all of that. Umm, railroads, workers, stocks going up. *The railroad was a big factor in.* . . .

The students who engaged in the analytic-writing task were guided by their own reformulation of the material. When they looked back to the passage, they did so to corroborate rather than find the ideas they wanted to write about and to select details to support and elaborate upon their points. The ideas remained the students' own. Unlike the other two writing groups, the analytic-writing group rarely relied on ideas or language drawn directly from the text. While these students dealt directly with a smaller proportion of the content in the original passage, they worked more extensively with the information they did use.

The beginning of Jill's think-aloud during an analytic-writing task illustrates the general approach to these tasks:

> Hmm . . . I'm rereading. Important reasons for occurring. . . . One of the reasons was the supply and demand, well, the law of demand. Right. Hmmm. . . . All right, so one example I can use is that demands grew greater, so supplies needed. . . . That's too confusing. I'm not going to do this one. Okay, the United States possessed many natural resources.

The fourth task asked students simply to "read and study" the passage. This can also be interpreted as a review condition, but one that lacks the focus provided by the writing tasks in the other two review conditions (comprehension questions and summary writing). This lack of focus led the students to wander somewhat in their approach, jumping from general summary to personal experience to tangentially related issues, pursuing none in great depth. Martha's think-aloud as she began to study shows her summarizing one of the factors in industrial growth:

> This passage mainly referred to the industrial growth of the country. And they give some general and specific factors of the growth. Like, ummm, immigration was an important factor for it. Since almost the beginning of the century, people have been coming to this country for better conditions of life. And they've been helping a lot in this growth.

Influence of Study Tasks on Recall

The study included three sets of measures of what students remembered about their reading: recall of content units, preservation of gist, and topic-specific knowledge.

Content Units Recalled

The patterns of recall of content units on the day following initial reading of the passage and five days later are summarized in table 16. If the tasks are ordered according to the degree to which they require focused, extended written responses (read and study < comprehension

Table 16

Overall Recall of Passage Content on Days Two and Six

| | | Adjusted Means, Percent Recalled | | |
| | | Compre-hension | | |
	(Pooled SD)	Read and Study ($n = 14$)	Ques-tions ($n = 17$)	Summary Writing ($n = 15$)	Analytic Writing ($n = 11$)
Day two	(5.5)	11.3	11.6	16.2	16.5
Day six	(5.1)	10.0	12.1	14.6	15.8

Analysis of Variance

	df	F	p
Between			
Task (linear)	1	5.93	.019
Task (deviations)	2	0.23	n.s.
Passage	1	6.01	.018
Task × passage	3	0.13	n.s.
Covariate	1	5.27	.026
Error	48		
Within			
Time	1	7.59	.008
Task (linear) × time	1	0.01	n.s.
Task (deviations) × time	2	0.72	n.s.
Passage × time	1	0.10	n.s.
Task × passage × time	3	3.60	.020
Error	49		

questions < summary writing < analytic writing), there is a significant linear effect for task ($p < .02$). Overall, the tasks involving writing led to better recall than did the read and study condition, and the extended writing tasks (summary and analysis) led to better recall than the more restricted writing task (comprehension questions). However, the proportion of content recalled for all four tasks was relatively low even at day two, ranging from a high of 17 percent for students in the analytic-writing condition to a low of 11 percent for those in the read-and-study condition.

On day six, overall recall dropped slightly (from 13.9 percent at day two to 13.1 percent, $p < .008$), with the two extended writing conditions continuing to do better than comprehension questions or read and study. (There was also a significant task × passage × time interaction reflecting a shift in relative ordering of the comprehension-question and the read-and-study conditions between the two passages at day six: on passage 1, students in the comprehension-question condition scored 1.1 percentage points lower than those in the read-and-study condition, while on passage 2, they scored 4.3 percentage points higher.)

Effect on Recall of Level in Content Hierarchy

Many previous studies have found that recall is influenced by the importance of the information in the overall structure of the passage. To examine the extent to which the importance of information might interact with recall in the four study conditions, we looked separately at recall in the top third, middle third, and bottom third of the content hierarchy in the original passage (table 17). As in previous studies, the overall tendency was that content higher in the passage structure was more likely to be recalled ($p < .002$), but the pattern was not particularly strong even at day two (12.4 percent for content from the top third compared with 8.2 percent for content from the bottom third). At all three levels, the effects of the writing tasks were roughly parallel to the effects on overall recall, though the scores for individual levels are less stable than the score for overall recall. The effects of most interest to the present study — the task by level interactions — were not significant.

Effect on Recall of Manipulating Content during Study Tasks

Of much more importance than level in the content hierarchy was whether a particular content unit had appeared in the writing completed as part of the original study task. Study two indicated that the number of words written while studying was significantly related to performance on post-test measures. In the present study, we were able to look directly at the relationships between content that was written about during the study task on day one and content that was recalled on days two and six. In table 18, the relevant results are summarized separately for content units that appeared in each student's study materials and for those that did not.

Overall, the students were much more likely to recall content units that they had directly included in their writing while studying the passages ($p < .001$). At day two, they recalled 38 percent of the content units they had directly manipulated, compared with only 5 percent of the content units not directly manipulated ($p < .001$). Further, the type of manipulation, as reflected in the nature of the study task, also had

Table 17

Recall by Level of Passage Structure on Days Two and Six

		Mean Percent Recalled				
	(Pooled SD)	All (N = 57)	Read and Study (n = 17)	Comprehension Questions (n = 15)	Summary Writing (n = 11)	Analytic Writing (n = 14)
Day two						
Top	(9.5)	12.4	8.0	13.8	13.4	14.4
Middle	(10.1)	11.3	12.6	9.6	12.1	14.3
Bottom	(6.4)	8.2	7.0	6.6	10.9	8.1
Day six						
Top	(7.4)	9.9	7.8	10.9	9.7	12.2
Middle	(8.2)	9.7	9.6	10.1	11.6	9.5
Bottom	(5.3)	7.0	4.7	5.3	8.0	11.0

Analysis of Variance

	df	F	p
Between			
Task (linear)	1	4.07	.044
Task (deviations)	2	0.41	n.s.
Passage	1	6.33	.015
Task × passage	3	0.15	n.s.
Covariate	1	5.38	.025
Error	48		
Within			
Time	1	7.97	.007
Time × task (linear)	1	0.00	n.s.
Time × task (deviations)	2	0.27	n.s.
Time × passage	1	0.01	n.s.
Time × task × passage	3	2.24	.094
Error (time)	49		
Level	2	6.91	.002
Level × task (linear)	1	1.39	n.s.
Level × task (deviations)	2	2.09	.129
Level × passage	2	6.41	.002
Level × task × passage	6	0.54	n.s.
Error (level)	98		
Time × level	2	0.50	n.s.
Time × level × task	6	1.50	.186
Time × level × passage	2	0.15	n.s.
Time × level × task × passage	6	0.42	n.s.
Error (time × level)	98		

Table 18

Recall by Manipulation of Passage Content on Days Two and Six

| | | Mean Percent Recalled | | |
	(Pooled SD)	All (N = 43)	Compre-hension Ques-tions (n = 17)	Summary Writing (n = 15)	Analytic Writing (n = 11)
Manipulated					
Day two	(17.2)	37.9	29.4	39.0	52.1
Day six	(18.4)	31.2	24.1	32.1	43.4
Not manipulated					
Day two	(3.8)	4.9	3.7	4.8	6.4
Day six	(3.8)	4.5	4.2	4.3	5.9

Analysis of Variance

	df	F	p
Between			
Task (linear)	1	17.48	.001
Task (deviations)	1	0.01	n.s.
Passage	1	1.60	n.s.
Task × passage	2	3.69	.035
Covariate	1	1.29	n.s.
Error	36		
Within			
Time	1	6.79	.013
Time × task (linear)	1	0.42	n.s.
Time × task (deviations)	1	0.33	n.s.
Time × passage	1	0.48	n.s.
Time × task × passage	2	1.21	n.s.
Error (time)	37		
Manipulation	1	223.99	.001
Manipulation × task (linear)	1	12.64	.001
Manipulation × task (deviations)	1	0.07	n.s.
Manipulation × passage	1	0.48	n.s.
Manipulation × task × passage	2	4.30	.021
Error (manipulation)	37		
Time × manipulation	1	5.33	.027
Time × manipulation × task	2	0.05	n.s.
Time × manipulation × passage	1	0.20	n.s.
Time × manipulation × task × passage	2	0.97	n.s.
Error (time × manipulation)	37		

a significant effect ($p < .001$), again in the predicted direction. At day two, students who completed comprehension questions recalled 29 percent of the content units that they included in their study task; students who summarized the passage recalled 39 percent; and students who completed an analytic-writing task recalled fully 50 percent. Recall of material not manipulated as part of the study task showed a similar trend, though even in the analytic-writing condition it averaged only 6 percent of the material.

These patterns of recall were remarkably stable even at the five-day retention test. The strongest effects continued to be associated with whether or not particular content units had been included in the study task: recall of manipulated content remained at 31 percent, compared with 5 percent for content that had not been manipulated. Similarly, the types of manipulation involved in analytic writing led to the best retention (43 percent), summary writing next (32 percent), and comprehension questions least (24 percent). Recall of content units not included in responses to the study tasks showed a similar ordering, though the amount recalled remained very small.

Capturing the Gist

It is possible to remember a goodly number of isolated facts from a passage without necessarily being able to relate those facts to one another in a systematic way. To assess this aspect of learning, we also rated each recall on a four-point scale reflecting the extent to which the gist or overall sense of the original text was captured. In table 19, mean scores are reported for recall of gist, as well as the percentage of recalls rated as "good" or "very good" at capturing the gist (3 or 4 on the scale).

As with the other measures discussed so far, ratings for gist showed a significant linear effect for task ($p < .04$), with students in the analytic-writing group doing best and those in the read-and-study and comprehension-question conditions doing least well. Students from the analytic-writing condition received considerably more "good" ratings for gist (73 percent) than did those who had completed comprehension questions (29 percent) or summary writing (31 percent). By day six the effects were weaker, though the two extended writing tasks continued to receive better ratings than either of the other two conditions.

Topic Knowledge

The third measure of the effects of the three study tasks was based on Langer's (1984b, 1984c) measure of topic-specific knowledge. This

Table 19

Ratings for Preserving Gist of Passage on Days Two and Six

	(Pooled SD)	Read and Study (n = 14)	Compre-hension Ques-tions (n = 17)	Summary Writing (n = 16)	Analytic Writing (n = 11)
Adjusted mean ratings (Pooled SD)					
Day two	(.8)	2.1	2.1	2.3	2.6
Day six	(.7)	2.1	2.1	2.3	2.5
Percent rated "good"					
Day two	23.1	29.4	31.3	72.7	
Day six	23.1	23.5	37.5	54.5	

Analysis of Variance

	df	F	p
Between			
Task (linear)	1	4.61	.037
Task (deviations)	2	0.25	n.s.
Passage	1	0.01	n.s.
Task × passage	3	0.01	n.s.
Covariate	1	2.53	.118
Error	48		
Within			
Time	1	0.01	n.s.
Task × time	3	0.24	n.s.
Passage × time	1	4.45	.040
Task × passage × time	3	2.19	.101
Error	49		

measure, which can be used whether or not the students have read a particular passage, was completed by all students three times (before reading, at day two, and at day six). At each administration, each student completed the measure for the assigned passage, as well as for the alternate (unread) passage. When the data were analyzed, the two passages were treated as separate replications. In each case, the students who had read the other passage were analyzed as an additional control condition of unrelated reading. That is, students who read "postwar Russia" also completed the "economic expansion" knowledge measure, and their responses to this measure over time were analyzed

Table 20

Topic-Specific Knowledge Scores on Days Two and Six

		Adjusted Means				
	(Pooled *SD*)	Unrelated Reading	Read and Study	Comprehension Questions	Summary Writing	Analytic Writing
Passage 1 concepts						
Day two	(4.7)	4.3	7.5	8.2	8.4	7.3
Day six	(3.1)	4.7	7.6	7.8	6.4	7.4
		(*n* = 46)	(*n* = 14)	(*n* = 14)	(*n* = 12)	(*n* = 7)
Passage 2 concepts						
Day two	(4.4)	4.9	3.7	9.4	7.3	12.1
Day six	(4.5)	4.7	3.7	9.2	6.3	11.8
		(*n* = 47)	(*n* = 11)	(*n* = 11)	(*n* = 14)	(*n* = 10)

Analysis of Variance

		Passage 1		Passage 2	
	df	*F*	*p*	*F*	*p*
Between					
Task (linear)	1	7.02	.010	15.10	.001
Task (deviations)	3	1.30	n.s.	2.11	.105
Covariate	1	52.72	.001	5.42	.022
Error	87				
Within					
Time	1	1.41	n.s.	1.70	.196
Task (linear) × time	1	4.83	.031	0.78	n.s.
Task (deviations) × time	3	1.66	.181	0.33	n.s.
Error	88				

as an "unrelated reading condition" in analyzing results for "postwar Russia." Conversely, in the analysis of "economic expansion," responses of students assigned to "postwar Russia" formed the unrelated reading group.

Results for this measure, summarized in table 20, reflect an interaction between passage and task. For passage 2, "economic expansion," simply reading the passage had no effect on students' passage-specific knowledge (mean scores of 4 at day two compared with mean scores of 5 in the unrelated reading condition). On the other hand, for passage 1, "postwar Russia," the read-and-study condition led to sharp gains in passage-specific knowledge (mean scores of 8 for the read-and-study condition versus 4 for the unrelated reading group). At day six, students in the analytic-writing condition performed considerably better than those in the other groups on passage 2 (with a mean of 12), but on passage 1 the parallel analytic-writing group did less well than the read-and-study or comprehension-question groups.

The results for gist may help us make sense of this pattern. At day two, gist scores for passage 1 were significantly higher than for passage 2. Students seem to have had a relatively easy time making sense of the account of recent Soviet history, and in turn quickly developed a cluster of passage-relevant information. The passage on economic factors in the post-Civil War era, on the other hand, was more difficult to understand. The focused attention provided by the three tasks that involved writing seems to have been more necessary in helping the students interrelate the information in the way reflected in the scores for gist, as well as in the passage-specific knowledge measure.

Results for day six, also summarized in table 20, reflect small decreases in passage-specific knowledge since day two. These decreases are relatively constant across tasks, except for the results for summary writing. For both passages, students in the summary-writing condition showed a somewhat sharper decrease in knowledge scores than did those in the other conditions.

Discussion

If we look across the series of studies presented in chapters 6 through 8, we can draw some general conclusions about the question with which we began: What is the role of writing in learning?

First, the more that content is manipulated, the more likely it is to be remembered and understood. In general, any kind of written response leads to better performance than does reading without writing. Within groups of students who complete the same tasks, students who write at greater length tend to perform better than students who write less, even after allowing for a general tendency for better students to do better at everything.

Second, the effects of writing tasks are greatest for the particular information focused upon during the writing. Our results suggest that the effects of writing on learning are highly specific and limited to information and ideas that are expressed again in the process of writing about them. We might have hoped that the process of writing about text material would lead to a more careful review of the whole text, forcing the students to review and reconceptualize all of its parts in the process of selecting what to write about. However, our results suggest that such effects are minimal at best. Rather than a generalized effect of writing on learning, there is a limited — and in some cases perhaps a limiting — one. Put another way, these results suggest that the particular writing task chosen may matter a great deal, depending upon a teacher's objectives.

Third, writing tasks differ in the breadth of information drawn upon and in the depth of processing of that information that they invoke. Thus note-taking, comprehension questions, and summarizing tasks, which focus attention across a text as a whole, have relatively generalized effects, though they lead to relatively superficial manipulation of the material being reviewed. They may be the tasks of choice when the purpose is to review a general body of information. Analytic-writing tasks, on the other hand, focus the writer more narrowly on a specific body of information. The results from the protocol analyses suggest that this attention is also more directly focused on the relationships that give structure and coherence to that information. In the context of learning from text, such tasks seem to lead to better retention of a smaller body of information. They will be the tasks of choice when the emphasis is on concepts and relationships in contexts where these relationships are more important than memory for a larger body of facts.

Finally, if content is familiar and relationships are well understood, writing may have no major effect at all. In these cases, simply reading the passage without any other attendant activity may be all that is needed to ensure comprehension and to remind readers of what they already know.

In these studies, we have made no attempt to separate the effects of writing from those of cognitive engagement. We suspect the two are inseparable and that the effects we have found for writing are a result of the kinds of engagement invoked by the different tasks. However, as educators we do not find the distinction particularly helpful. Writing seems to be at least one very useful way that teachers can orchestrate the kinds of cognitive engagement that leads to academic learning. While similar kinds of engagement can be invoked using other instructional techniques such as group or class discussion, writing activities are easier to plan and execute than many of the alternatives, and they have the advantage of maximizing the likelihood that all students, not only the most vocal, will be involved.

The results of our study of learning from writing, like those from the studies of individual classrooms, do not yield any simple prescriptions. Different types of written tasks promote different kinds of learning, and choosing among them will depend upon the teacher's goals for a particular lesson or a particular course. Although they do not yield simple prescriptions for teaching, the results of our studies are generally encouraging: they suggest that the choices we make as teachers can be reasoned choices, reflecting the kinds of engagement with the subject matter that we value most for particular groups of students at particular points in time. Writing across the curriculum is perhaps too simplistic a concept, but our results provide good support for the underlying premise that writing tasks have a significant role to play in all areas of academic study.

The argument so far has had two parts. In the studies of teaching, we examined how writing activities function in a variety of subject areas and concluded that such activities are often limited and perhaps trivialized by their assimilation to old routines of teaching. In the studies of student learning, we have argued that the different types of writing activities have different effects on learning — that writing is not writing is not writing. Given these twin findings, do we have any alternative that might allow writing activities a broader role in fostering students' engagement in more complex and sophisticated reasoning? Sketching that alternative will be our task in the next chapter.

IV Conclusions

9 Learning from Writing in the Secondary School: Accomplishing Our Goals

We began this project with two goals: first, to extend research knowledge about the effects of writing on content learning and, second, to develop models of thoughtful and thought-provoking writing activities that would work in a variety of subject-area classrooms. We achieved these goals, and more.

Learning from Writing

From the series of studies of learning and writing, we gained a more complete understanding of the ways that writing works in support of learning. Across the studies, there is clear evidence that activities involving writing (*any* of the many sorts of writing we studied) lead to better learning than activities involving reading and studying only. Writing assists learning. Beyond that, we learned that writing is not writing is not writing; different kinds of writing activities lead students to focus on different kinds of information, to think about that information in different ways, and in turn to take quantitatively and qualitatively different kinds of knowledge away from their writing experiences.

Short-answer study questions, for example, lead students to focus on particular items of information either located in the text or implied by it. When completing writing tasks of this sort, students often look for the information in the textbook or in class notes and "transcribe" it directly onto the paper — from text to paper, with the student writer as conduit. Little rethinking of the material usually takes place. However, because this kind of activity usually includes questions about many different aspects of the material being studied, it generally leads to short-term recall of a good deal of specific information.

In contrast, analytic writing leads to a more thoughtful focus on a smaller amount of information. While fewer ideas are considered, they are dealt with in more complex ways; ideas are linked and understanding is reconstrued. Although less information is likely to be remembered immediately, over time this information is longer lived.

135

Why does this happen? Results from our analyses of think-aloud protocols gathered as students completed in-class as well as experimenter-prepared writing tasks indicate that some tasks lead students to more complex manipulations of the material they are writing about, while other tasks lead them to move more rapidly — and more superficially — through larger quantities of material. And when information is manipulated in more complex ways, it tends to be better understood and better remembered. Our studies show further that it is the particular information the writer focuses on that is affected; related material from the same passage is remembered much less well.

Where does that leave us? While writing helps learning, it is important for teachers to be selective about the kinds of writing activities they ask their students to engage in, depending on the kinds of learning they are seeking. Analytic writing leads to a focus on selective parts of the text, to deeper reasoning about less information. Summary writing and note-taking, in contrast, lead to a focus on the whole text in more comprehensive but more superficial ways. Short-answer study questions focus attention on particular information, with little attention to overall relationships. Each type of writing and each kind of learning has its place in schools, particularly when writing is used selectively for particular purposes. The ability to select appropriate writing activities as well as the ability to engage successfully in them will, we think, enhance students' thinking and reasoning.

Writing in the Classroom

We also learned a great deal from our studies of teaching. First, we learned that writing activities can be developed to support the content goals in a variety of high school subject classes. Although each of the teachers we worked with took a somewhat different approach to the curriculum and had somewhat different instructional goals, writing activities in each of the classrooms fit these goals and also provided the students with opportunities to use writing as a means to learn content.

In working with the teachers, we learned that subject-area writing can be used productively in three primary ways: (1) to gain relevant knowledge and experience in preparing for new activities; (2) to review and consolidate what is known or has been learned; and (3) to reformulate and extend ideas and experiences. Our analyses of the students' papers and their self-reports indicated that writing used to reformulate and extend knowledge led to more complex reasoning than did the other types of writing; review writing led to the least.

While all three types of writing activities had a place in each of the content classrooms we studied, review writing predominated. Although review writing works well to help students rethink and clarify new learnings, little review writing was used for this purpose. Instead, it was used to grade the students on newly learned material. This approach, we found, was an outgrowth of the teachers' need to evaluate the effectiveness of their teaching as well as to assess their students' learning. In most cases, review writing provided an easy mechanism for that evaluation. Writing was most effectively used to enhance student learning only when the teachers' criteria for judging that learning changed from the accuracy of students' recitations to the adequacy of their thinking.

Evaluation continued, but its nature changed as the teachers began to judge the effectiveness of student learning on the basis of the quality of their ideas. Then it became possible to introduce a variety of in-process writing activities as well as "think papers" in which there were no clearly right or wrong answers, but in which the students' progress toward a deeper understanding of the material was evident. And it was this progress toward deeper understanding that served as evidence for learning.

While results from the studies of writing and learning reinforced our belief that writing can be a useful aid to learning in high school course work, the classroom studies highlighted the many difficulties that arise when process-oriented writing activities are incorporated into traditional classrooms. Without new models for evaluating student learning, teachers will continue to rely on old indicators and, in doing so, abort the deeper process of instructional change they meant to embrace.

Notions of Instruction

We can better understand the teachers' notions of instruction if we place them in the context of more general views of literacy instruction and literacy learning. Notions of literacy and what it means to be a literate individual have taken on different meanings at many points in our history (Resnick and Resnick, 1977). Throughout the 1900s, however, approaches to literacy instruction have remained relatively stable, as have more general beliefs about teaching and learning. During the first half of the twentieth century, issues in reading and writing instruction were essentially issues of curriculum: what should be taught and how to evaluate the success of that teaching. Early analyses were concerned with describing the skills students lacked in order to define simultaneously the skills that should be included in the curriculum (see Langer, 1984a).

Implicit in this model was an orientation that treated the purposes guiding the reading or writing activity as essentially irrelevant. That is, the activities themselves and the work that resulted from having engaged in those activities received the focus, while the functional aspects of the activities were largely ignored. This resulted in a variety of practice exercises that tended to become separated from the more complete and purposeful activities to which they initially belonged. Through the years, classroom approaches to the teaching of predetermined content and skills changed. At times the skills were thought to be best taught out of context, at other times within the context of larger, meaningful units of text. At times the focus was on diagnostic testing to individualize each student's program of subskill learning, and at other times all students were thought to benefit from exposure to the entire developmental sequence of skill training.

Although differing in their implementation, these approaches all viewed the teacher as a provider of information. They also relied heavily upon testing to determine what the students needed to know. The teacher's craft was one of knowing the range of skills, diagnosing what the students still needed to learn, providing instruction directed at the missing skills, and testing to see if the instruction had been effective.

This version of curriculum is based on an industrial metaphor (Callahan, 1962) and is often accompanied by a fairly complex management plan that controls the sequence of diagnostic testing and provides appropriate instruction, evaluation, and reteaching. The materials and activities developed to accompany such a program are structured to provide students with myriad opportunities to practice what they cannot already do. With some shifts in emphasis across the years, this version of curriculum dominated instruction throughout the first half of the twentieth century, was at the base of the curriculum reform movement in the 1960s, and, despite the process- and context-oriented research of the past two decades, continues to undergird contemporary approaches to schooling, including the approaches of the teachers we studied.

Though persistent and widespread, this model of teaching militates against many of our goals for writing and learning. It emphasizes the teacher as transmitter of knowledge, rather than the students as active agents who must interpret and reinterpret what they are learning; it emphasizes testing and evaluation, rather than work in progress; and

industrial model

it emphasizes declarative rather than procedural knowledge (knowing *that* rather than knowing *how*). To summarize bluntly, given traditional notions of instruction, it may be impossible to implement successfully the approaches we have championed.

Toward an Alternative View of Writing Instruction

This interpretation of the results of our studies has led us to develop an alternative view of effective instruction. In this view, rather than providing information and evaluating what students have learned, effective writing instruction provides carefully structured support or *scaffolding* as students undertake new and more difficult tasks. In the process of completing those tasks, students internalize information and strategies relevant to the tasks, learning the concepts and skills they will need in order eventually to undertake similar tasks on their own. In developing this model, we are concerned not so much with psychological models of learning as with the context of the classroom. The model posits a view of instruction that is contextually embedded and that articulates with day-to-day practice as well as with what we have learned about psychology and language learning. It offers a bridge between the worlds of theory and practice.

Studies of Learning

The view that we have adopted grows out of a more general view of language learning, one that has been heavily influenced by the work of both Vygotsky and Bruner. Vygotsky (1962, 1978, 1981) focuses on language as a social and communicative activity. He argues that higher level skills are the result of the child's learning of social-functional relationships; in becoming literate, children internalize the structures of socially meaningful literacy activities. Interactive events are at the heart of literacy learning. They involve the child as an active learner in a setting where an adult guides the child's progress through the learning task. Through successive guided experiences, children come to develop their own self-regulatory abilities. Thus approaches that are initially mediated socially are eventually internalized and become part of the repertoire of the individual.

Similarly, Bruner views the adult-child tutorial relationship as critical to language learning (Wood, Bruner, and Ross, 1976). He uses the term *scaffolding* to describe the tutorial assistance provided by the adult who knows how to control those elements that are beyond the child's capabilities. Bruner views language as providing the basis for concept formation, as a tool for cognitive growth (Bruner, Oliver, Greenfield, and others, 1966). Further, he sees writing as a powerful tool essential for thinking (1973), and schooling as promoting the growth of reasoning abilities through training in the mastery of written language. Written language, he believes, is particularly important in encouraging cognitive growth because it is abstract — the referent is not present as it is during many forms of oral discourse. The language of school is particularly important in developing abstract literacy skills, requiring students to go beyond concrete facts and to deal with abstractions.

Both Vygotsky and Bruner see language learning as growing out of a communicative relationship where the adult helps the child understand as well as complete new tasks. These authors also see literacy as encouraging the kinds of thinking and reasoning that can support higher levels of cognitive development.

Our general approach to the study of literacy is to treat literacy learning as an extension of these language-learning processes and to embed our analyses in more general frameworks of language learning (Langer and Applebee, 1986).

Studies of Instruction

The power of these early language-learning strategies is attested to by the rapid growth of language in the young child, but only recently have we begun to understand these strategies and more recently still to use them as a framework for examining instruction. Cazden (1979), summarizing recent research on discourse learning, proposes Bruner's studies of parent-child interaction as a starting point for a new instructional model. In our own papers, we have been developing the concept of instructional scaffolding as an important component of effective literacy instruction, functioning much as the adult in the adult-child pairs: simplifying the situation, clarifying the structure, helping the student accomplish tasks that would otherwise be too difficult, and providing the framework and rules of procedure that will gradually be internalized until the instructional support is no longer needed (Applebee and Langer, 1983; Langer, 1984a; Langer and Applebee, 1984, 1986).

Instructional Scaffolding

Similar to these patterns, the most successful instruction observed in our project occurred when the students and the teacher had a shared understanding of the specific goals of an instructional activity, as well as a shared sense that the activity required a collaborative interaction if it was to be completed successfully. These observations have led us to elaborate our notion of instructional scaffolding as an alternative model to traditional approaches to literacy instruction. In its present form, the model falls short of a complete theory of instruction, serving instead as a metaphor that captures the most important dimensions of change that are needed for effective literacy instruction. In our earlier papers, we proposed five components of effective instructional scaffolding. Even though our vocabulary keeps changing, we have labeled these components *ownership, appropriateness, support, collaboration,* and *internalization.* We will summarize each of them briefly, highlighting the ways that they relate to previous studies, as well as the ways that they appeared in the classrooms we studied here.

Ownership

Effective instructional tasks must allow room for students to have something of their own to say in their writing. Students must see the point of the task, beyond simple obedience to the teacher's demands. It is this sense of purposefulness that will integrate the various parts of the task into a coherent whole, providing a sense of direction. The focus must be on what is being accomplished through writing if the student is to learn procedures to carry out those purposes.

In practice, this focus is often neglected. The majority of writing tasks require recitation of previous learning, allowing the student little room to claim ownership for what is being written. Even when process supports such as brainstorming activities or multiple drafts are provided, these supports are often seen by the students as separate activities unrelated to the writing that the process activities were meant to support.

In the present study, we have seen how difficult it is for teachers to allow room for such ownership to develop. In the three science classes, the demands for accuracy and knowledge of the appropriate content kept shifting the teachers' focus toward recitation, so much so that in Julian Bardolini's class even a learning log eventually became a context for recitation rather than interpretation of the day's activities. In Jane Martin's social studies class, her concern with protecting her students from error led her to provide so much structure that there was little room left for the students to claim their own point of view, even though she felt that developing their own opinions was an important and continuing goal. In Jack Graves's English class, ownership was limited to "motivational" tasks, personal writing that was kept separate from literary studies. It was never clear that Graves saw a place for students' own interpretations in literary study, at least not if there were any possibility that those interpretations might vary from those sanctioned by tradition.

Appropriateness

Effective instructional tasks will build on literacy and thinking skills the students already have, helping them to accomplish tasks that they could not otherwise complete on their own. In Vygotsky's (1962) terms, instruction should be aimed "not so much at the ripe, but at the ripening functions." (More specifically, Vygotsky argues that instruction should be addressed at the zone of proximal development, defined essentially as tasks that a learner can complete with appropriate help but would be unable to complete unaided.) Such approaches work only when the interaction builds on the language resources that students already have, stretching them to new and more complex contexts. When the stretch is too far, the dialogue falls apart and progress is resumed only when the teacher redefines the task in terms closer to the students' understanding of the situation.

Again, our studies of writing instruction suggest that this principle is more violated than observed. When students are asked to undertake new tasks, the tasks are too often not set in the context of skills and knowledge the students already have. This manifests itself in two ways: as the assumption that if students are simply given a topic to write about, they will somehow know how to do it; or in the assumption that every element of a new task must be taught from scratch, as though the students had no resources to draw upon already.

The teachers in the present study were continually amazed by what their students were able to do when challenged with new tasks. Graves's impromptu themes, Bush's and Moss's "What If . . ." assignments, and Martin's inference papers all represented tasks their students were ready for and to which they responded well. On the other hand, the teachers in their enthusiasm for new approaches to writing sometimes stepped beyond what the students could manage even with guidance, and the assignments collapsed in frustration and occasional anger.

Support

To be an effective vehicle for learning, instructional tasks must make the structure of the activity clear and must guide the student through it in a way that will provide effective strategies for use in other contexts. Put another way, the task must support a natural sequence of thought and language, providing effective routines for the students to internalize.

Support of this sort is one of the most consistent features in studies of effective instruction — the student learns to do new language tasks by being led through them in the context of a supportive dialogue. This ensures that skill learning includes a sense of the appropriate contexts for use; new procedures and routines are embedded in the contexts they serve, rather than being presented as isolated components that may or may not be seen as relevant. Embedded in this way, their use may be highlighted by the teacher's commentary, but this is very different from teaching the procedures as skills out of context.

In practice, writing instruction is usually organized around skills to be learned rather than purposes to be accomplished. Models of curriculum lay stress on hierarchies of skills to be learned, often in elaborate scope and sequence charts, and teaching and testing emphasize those skills — the parts rather than the whole. Although recent attention to process models of instruction seems to be moving toward teaching that is responsive to "natural" stages in the writing task, very little of the process approach has made its way into classrooms. Most students write little, and when they do write, the writing usually involves a first-and-final draft of a page or less, produced in one class period in response to an assignment that specifies an appropriate length, topic, due date — and little more.

Again, the present study contains many examples of how appropriate support can extend students' capabilities and enrich their learning. When Janet Bush asked her students to create a new animal, she provided the structure and guidance that made it possible for them to do so successfully. Julian Bardolini's guide questions for his daily journals, Jack Graves's detailed preliminary discussions of the formal essays he required, and Jane Martin's "formula paper" all offered similar structure, helping the students complete a task while they were learning the skills that would eventually allow them to complete similar tasks on their own. The last two examples illustrate a natural tension, however, between support and ownership: the craft of teaching is in part a process of finding the proper balance between providing enough support and taking too much control.

Collaboration

At the heart of the teacher-student relationship is a bond of collaboration. The teacher's role is one of helping students toward new learning, rather than of testing the adequacy of new learning. This role is obvious in the interaction between parent and child, where the adult assumes that the child has something that she or he wants to say or do and works with the child to carry this through to completion. The adult's repertoire of devices includes modeling, extension, rephrasing, questioning, praise, and correction, but they are employed in the service of the task (book reading, peek-a-boo, puzzle building), rather than to judge the child's performance.

Teachers' roles in writing instruction are rarely collaborative, however. Much more frequently, the role is one of evaluation, which is usually tied to previous learning, not to learning in progress. We speak of cheating rather than of help, and grades rather than ways to solve a writing problem. Our studies show that the role of teacher-as-evaluator permeates almost all classroom exchanges, written and oral alike.

Adopting a collaborative rather than an evaluative stance was one of the most difficult things for the teachers in our study to achieve. Their concerns with evaluation were deeply ingrained in the structure of their classrooms as well as in the schools and districts within which they taught. Some of the teachers never managed to shift their focus; others did so by establishing specific contexts separate from the ongoing stream of classroom activity. Thus some of Kathryn Moss's most successful activities were her "practice conclusions," which were optional and not graded because they were work in progress.

Internalization

As new learnings mature, they become internalized as part of the student's own repertoire. They move from the interpersonal setting of instruction to the inner world of knowing and remembering. Cazden (1979) and Griffin and Cole (1984) have pointed out that the term *scaffolding* appears more static than the concept is meant to imply. It is a peculiar kind of scaffold we mean — one that self-destructs as the child internalizes its features, allowing the student to complete similar tasks without further help. (However, the teacher-student relationship leaves open the opportunity for new interactions to occur with whatever new scaffolding is needed.)

In our instructional practices, we too often forget to let the scaffolding self-destruct. In one part of our study of writing instruction, we analyzed popular textbooks in seven subject areas and found few differences in the writing activities suggested between the ninth and the eleventh grades and no differences in the kinds of activities suggested over the course of a year in individual texts (Applebee,

Langer, et al., 1984). There was no transfer of control from teacher (or textbook) to student in response to the learning that was presumably taking place. When something works well, we tend to keep using it without being sensitive to whether the students still need the kind of support that the activity was initially meant to provide.

This view of instruction permits a fusion of the need for direct instruction in new skills with the recent concern about reading and writing processes. The critical feature is that the instruction take place in a context where student as well as teacher has an active role to play in the writing activity. Room must be allowed for a shared exchange of ideas between teacher and student and an underlying understanding about their roles and goals — who needs the help, who gives the help, what help is needed, and why.

When instruction is approached in this way, student and teacher roles necessarily change and, along with them, the nature of lessons and learning. Instruction takes on a different face that requires new uses of materials and new ways to assess whether learning has taken place. In this model of instruction, the teacher retains the role of planner and initiator of classroom activities. However, the activities planned need to provide scope for the students to develop their own purposes rather than simply providing responses to fit into the teacher's predetermined framework.

The notion of instructional scaffolding provides both a framework for analyzing ongoing instruction and a metaphor that teachers may find helpful in reformulating their practice. Unlike the notions of curriculum that underlie current practice, instructional scaffolding leaves room for encouraging reasoning of a higher order as well as for the basic skills. It may also offer a way to integrate recent scholarly attention to reading and writing processes with the practical and pressing concerns of the classroom.

Changing Practice

New views of instruction are not likely to replace more traditional views without well-orchestrated support for change on the part of the teacher, the school administration, and the general public. Although we began our studies with the relatively simple agenda of developing models of effective uses of writing in a variety of secondary school subject areas, we ended with a recognition of the many institutional and professional constraints that influenced what the teachers were able to do.

Institutional Constraints

Testing and Evaluation

As we have seen, testing plays an integral part in the model of curriculum that dominates in most classrooms. Test construction is generally guided by what the test writers think *should* be taught. Tests are used to diagnose the knowledge already attained and to identify what to teach next, as well as to evaluate the success of the teaching.

Evaluation of student learning is also deeply embedded in the exercises and activities that accompany commercially published textbooks and curriculum materials. In addition, schools and districts tend to rely on formal testing programs to monitor educational progress and evaluate the effectiveness of educational programs. Dorr-Bremme and Herman (1986) found that in American secondary schools 12 to 13 percent of available instructional time in the subjects they studied was devoted to testing — roughly one test in each subject every three to four days.

The classrooms we studied mirrored this general pattern: tests in their various forms were frequent, and ongoing work was evaluated as an indication of previous learning. We have discussed at some length how the teachers struggled with the general problem of evaluating ongoing work and how inhibiting this struggle was to the process of change. Many of the most interesting activities were successful only because the teachers removed them from the stream of evaluation, treating them as drafts or work in progress or as extra-credit assignments that would receive points for completion rather than grades.

Less obvious but no less real was the tension generated by more formal testing such as the school and district examinations that students faced in most subjects. As in most school districts, these tests were tailored to the district curricula and focused on information that could be tested in easily scored, multiple-choice formats. The tests emphasized breadth of coverage rather than depth of understanding. As we have seen in our studies of student learning, there is a real tension between depth and breadth of learning: activities that focus on a deeper understanding and more complex thinking usually focus on a narrower band of information. In planning their curricula, the teachers in our study often had to choose between these goals: to ask the students to write at any length about one topic meant a trade-off of time that could have been devoted to other topics. In her interview with us after the first year of work, Jane Martin commented on the effect this constraint had had:

> The district competency test had seventy-five multiple-choice items. The distribution for my class was strange; I had them skip some items. They skipped all the questions on Japan, which we never got to. But they learned better things as a result of the writing: (1) they learned how to think a little better; (2) they learned how to organize a little better; and (3) they learned better how to raise questions and judge answers [about the topics we did study].

The district examination valued coverage rather than depth of understanding and thus was at odds with the choices Martin had made. The influence of these tests was kept to a minimum only because of the professional self-assurance of the teachers we worked with. They believed in what they were doing and were secure enough with their colleagues and supervisors to accept the risk that their students' results might have a "strange distribution" as long as the students also "learned better things."

Administrative support at the department, school, and district level is critical if teachers in general are to accept such goals. Instructional change does not take place when it is in conflict with institutional values, particularly as those values are expressed in the system of testing. Although many school administrators claim to desire instructional programs that foster higher levels of thinking in content learning, the tests they mandate often evaluate the more superficial and unintegrated learning supported by less complex writing and thinking.

Thus new criteria need to be developed to evaluate more complex forms of student learning, and these criteria need to become part of traditional testing programs. Including essays as a regular and expected part of all examinations would help in this regard, although they would have to be accompanied by innovative marking procedures. Unfortunately, the easiest way to grade essays is to develop rubrics that give credit for specific information included in the writing. But if essays are graded by such rubrics, they reward exactly the same sorts of learning as do the multiple choice examinations they are meant to replace. Teachers of English have come to rely increasingly on general impression or primary trait scoring as ways to deal with such problems — methods of evaluation that turn attention toward the effectiveness and structure of the argument as a whole rather than toward the parts out of which it is built. It should be possible to modify such approaches to reflect the quality of students' reasoning about specific subject matter, striking a balance between the power of the underlying conceptualization and the accuracy and breadth of the supporting detail. Such alternative ways to evaluate student learning and to judge program effectiveness at the district level would serve as powerful support for teachers to use more thoughtful approaches to instruction and evaluation in their own classes.

Textbooks and Materials

Another institutional factor that constrained the approaches the teachers were able to adopt was the quality of the textbooks and instructional materials available to them. Virtually without exception, the materials available provided piecemeal and inadequate models of teaching and learning. In working with us, none of the teachers could turn to the materials already available for helpful suggestions or new ideas; they had to create each activity from scratch. Even with the support provided by the project staff, this was a slow and laborious process requiring more time and energy than most teachers can afford to invest. Rather than new approaches, the activities in the commercially available materials reflected an eclectic and haphazard collection of old suggestions, focusing for the most part on breadth rather than depth of coverage and on evaluating what students had learned rather than on helping them in the process of learning.

The problems in the textbook materials operated at two levels. On one level, the activities and exercises emphasized review and evaluation. On another level, the textbooks themselves were poor models of writing and thinking within the disciplines they represented. Rather than conveying the excitement of scientific or historical inquiry, the textbooks in those subjects served more as reference guides to scientific or historical information. They were dull and gave little sense of the organizing concepts that might matter within the discipline. The teachers were aware of the difficulty and devoted much of their teaching time to reviewing ideas that students should have gotten from their textbooks. To a greater extent than should have been necessary, they devoted class time to creating rather than reinforcing and extending frameworks for understanding the subject matter. The teachers we chose to work with were able to do this quite well, but one must wonder how teachers with less experience or background in their fields can manage.

Conditions of Instruction

The third set of institutional constraints stemmed from the conditions of instruction. One of the most frequent concerns about asking students to write is how to manage the paper load. When teachers meet five classes daily, each with thirty or more students, the concern is legitimate. The teachers in our study had no control over the conditions under which they taught, but they did find their own solutions to the paper load. These solutions took a number of forms, including limiting the length of the assignments, focusing on content rather than on spelling and grammar, relying on peer response to early drafts, and postponing grading until the final stages. At other times, student papers were used as the basis of class discussion, relieving the need for collecting and reviewing them.

At the same time, these solutions raised various kinds of tension, foremost among them the teachers' concern that their actions would be misunderstood. As one teacher said, "If I send work home without marking all of the spelling errors, will the parents think I don't know any better?"

Counterbalancing these concerns was a gradual discovery that well-constructed writing tasks lead to interesting writing, which in turn can reduce the burden of responding to the papers. Jane Martin expressed it well:

> I actually had fewer papers to grade during the project time —
> not so many objective things to grade. Overall it probably took
> more time though, because the writing took longer. But I enjoyed
> reading it; I even look forward to reading their papers. That was
> a change.

The teachers who adopted flexible approaches to the paper load were those who became most comfortable assigning writing to their classes. They used preparatory writing as the basis for discussion, review writing as preparation for papers and self-assessments as well as for personal journals and learning logs, and writing to reformulate and extend as part of work in progress. Each type of writing was also used as the basis for peer responses as well as for whole class discussions. Writing, the teachers learned, can be for the *student* as well as for the *teacher*.

Professional Constraints

The final constraint on adopting new approaches stemmed from a general failure of the teaching profession to provide teachers with clear conceptualizations of the nature of writing specific to their disciplines. While teachers can easily recognize (and reward) correct information, they have more trouble articulating the rhetoric or the rules of evidence that govern effective argument within their particular disciplines.

If teachers are to help students think more deeply about the subjects they are studying, then we must begin to articulate the components of effective discourse in particular disciplines. Further, if writing is to play a meaningful role in subjects other than English, then the teachers of those subjects will need to have a conception of writing specific to their disciplines, one that emphasizes what is unique about writing (and thinking) in their subject, rather than one that emphasizes ways in which such activities will foster the work of the English teacher.

Although broad discourse purposes or uses of language are common to the various high school subjects, the similarity in purpose may also mask very important differences in how these purposes are achieved. These differences are likely to involve very fundamental concepts — notions of causality and proof, of evidence or warrants for claims, of assumptions that can be taken for granted, and of premises that must be made explicit and defended. Such concepts may lie at the heart of learning to write effectively about a particular subject area, as well as at the heart of the development of the higher level thinking skills that so few students seem to achieve.

Our studies of effective teachers have highlighted the extent to which our understanding of writing skills has focused at the level of generic purposes and has ignored the specific content domain within which students are writing. In retrospect, this focus has contributed to two widely held assumptions that we sought to challenge in the present study: (1) that writing is primarily the job of the English teacher, who should be teaching the generic strategies; and (2) that writing within other subjects has no fundamental relationship to the teaching of those subjects. Given these assumptions, to the extent that writing is emphasized it will be only as a help to the English teacher or as a diagnostic tool to see what students have learned.

However, another way of viewing the classroom can transform the role of writing. This is to view the classroom as a community of scholars (or of scholars and apprentices) with its own rules of evidence and procedures for carrying the discussion forward. Students must learn, then, not only the "basic facts" around which discussion is structured, but the legal and illegal ways in which those facts can be mustered in the disciplinary community defined by that classroom. This discussion will be partly oral, in the presentations and interactions that make up the dialogue of instruction; but the opportunity for individuals to make extended contributions during class discussion are necessarily limited. Writing then becomes a primary and necessary vehicle for practicing the ways of organizing and presenting ideas that are most appropriate to a particular subject area. In such a view, writing, rather than being an aid to the English teacher, becomes a major vehicle for conceptual learning in all of the academic disciplines.

Final Thoughts

We began this book by stating our belief that the effective teaching of writing is an essential component of school programs in general. Much beyond the English classroom, writing supports more complex thinking and learning about the subjects that students are expected to learn. We also provided evidence from recent studies that the amount and complexity of the writing required in American schools gives cause for concern.

The studies we presented in the major portion of this book have helped to answer some of the very basic questions we set for ourselves. Written language does indeed make a contribution to content learning and it can support the more complex kind of reasoning that is increasingly necessary for successful performance in our complex technological and information-based culture. It becomes essential, then, to make clear and effective writing in all school subjects a central objective of the school curriculum. If this objective is to be met, however, policy makers, administrators, and teachers alike will need to work together to reward thoughtful argument over simple recitation, to judge the effectiveness of schooling by standards that take into account how students reason and learn about the subject matter in addition to how much they know, and to communicate these expectations clearly and forcefully to the students themselves and to the community at large.

References

Anderson, R. C., and Biddle, B. W. (1975). On asking people questions about what they are reading. In G. Bower (Ed.), *The psychology of learning and motivation, Vol. 9.* New York: Academic Press.

Anderson, V., Bereiter, C., and Smart, D. (1979). *Activation of semantic networks in writing: Teaching students how to do it themselves.* The Ontario Institute for Studies in Education. Paper presented at annual meeting of AERA, 1980.

Applebee, A. N. (1977). Writing across the curriculum: The London projects. *English Journal, 66*(9), 81–85.

Applebee, A. N. (1981). *Writing in the secondary school.* Urbana, IL: National Council of Teachers of English.

Applebee, A. N. (1982). Writing and learning in school settings. In P. M. Nystrand (Ed.), *What writers know: The language, process, and structure of written discourse.* New York: Academic Press.

Applebee, A. N. (1984). Writing and reasoning. *Review of Educational Research, 54*(4), 577–596.

Applebee, A. N. (1986). Problems in process approaches: Toward a reconceptualization of process instruction. In A. R. Petrosky and D. Bartholomae (Eds.), *The teaching of writing.* 85th Yearbook. Chicago: National Society for the Study of Education.

Applebee, A. N., and Langer, J. A. (1983). Instructional scaffolding: Reading and writing as natural language activities. *Language Arts, 60*(2), 168–175.

Applebee, A. N., Langer, J. A., et al. (1984). *Contexts for learning to write.* Norwood, NJ: Ablex.

Applebee, A. N., Langer, J. A., and Mullis, I. V. S. (1985). *The reading report card: Progress toward excellence in our schools.* National Assessment of Educational Progress. Princeton, NJ: Educational Testing Service.

Applebee, A. N., Langer, J. A., and Mullis, I. V. S. (1986a). *Writing: Trends across the decade, 1974–84.* National Assessment of Educational Progress. Princeton, NJ: Educational Testing Service.

Applebee, A. N., Langer, J. A., and Mullis, I. V. S. (1986b). *The writing report card: Writing achievement in American schools.* National Assessment of Educational Progress. Princeton, NJ: Educational Testing Service.

Applebee, A. N., Langer, J. A., and Mullis, I. V. S. (1987). *Learning to be literate in America: Reading, writing, and reasoning.* National Assessment of Educational Progress. Princeton, NJ: Educational Testing Service.

Barnett, J., Di Vesta, F. J., and Rogozinski, J. T. (1981). What is learned in note taking? *Journal of Educational Psychology, 73*(2), 181–192.

Bereiter, C., and Scardamalia, M. (1982). From conversation to composition: The role of instruction in a developmental process. In R. Glaser (Ed.), *Advances in instructional psychology (Vol. 2)*. Hillsdale, NJ: Erlbaum.

Bereiter, C., Scardamalia, M., Anderson, V., and Smart, D. (1979). *An experiment in teaching abstract planning in writing*. The Ontario Institute for Studies in Education. Paper presented at annual meeting of AERA, 1980.

Boyer, E. L. (1983). *High school: A report on secondary education in America*. New York: Harper and Row.

Bretzing, B. H., and Kulhavy, R. W. (1979). Notetaking and depth of processing. *Contemporary Educational Psychology, 4*(2), 145–153.

Bretzing, B. H., and Kulhavy, R. W. (1981). Note-taking and passage style. *Journal of Educational Psychology, 73*(2), 242–250.

Britton, J., Burgess, T., Martin, N., McLeod, A., and Rosen, H. (1975). *The development of writing abilities (11–18)*. London: Macmillan Education.

Bruner, J. S. (1971). *The relevance of education*. New York: Norton.

Bruner, J. S. (1978). The role of dialogue in language acquisition. In A. Sinclair et al. (Eds.), *The child's conception of language* (241–256). New York: Springer-Verlag.

Bruner, J. S., Oliver, R. R., Greenfield, P. M., et al. (1966). *Studies in cognitive growth: A collaboration at the Center for Cognitive Studies*. New York: Wiley.

Callahan, R. E. (1962). *Education and the cult of efficiency: A study of the social forces that have shaped the administration of the public schools*. Chicago: University of Chicago Press.

Cazden, C. (1979). Peekaboo as an instructional model: Discourse development at home and at school. *Papers and Reports on Child Language Development, 17*, 1–19.

Cole, M., and Griffin, P. (1985, February). *A socio-historical approach to the study of remediation*. Laboratory of Comparative Human Development, University of California–San Diego. Unpublished manuscript.

Craik, F. I. M., and Lockhart, R. S. (1972). Levels of processing: A framework for memory research. *Journal of Verbal Learning and Verbal Behavior, 11*, 671–684.

Di Vesta, F. J., and Gray, G. S. (1972). Listening and notetaking. *Journal of Educational Psychology, 63*, 8–14.

Di Vesta, F. J., Schultz, C. B., and Dangel, T. R. (1973). Passage organization and imposed learning strategies in comprehension and recall of connected discourse. *Memory and Cognition, 1*(4), 471–476.

Dorr-Bremme, D., and Herman, J. L. (1986). *Assessing student achievement: A profile of classroom practices*. Monograph Series in Evaluation No. 11. Los Angeles: University of California–Los Angeles, Center for the Study of Evaluation.

Fisher, J. L., and Harris, M. R. (1973). Effect of notetaking and review on recall. *Journal of Educational Psychology, 65*, 321–325.

Flower, L. S., and Hayes, J. R. (1980a). The cognition of discovery: Defining a rhetorical problem. *College Composition and Communication, 31*, 21–32.

Flower, L. S., and Hayes, J. R. (1980b). The dynamics of composing: Making plans and juggling constraints. In L. W. Gregg and E. R. Steinberg (Eds.), *Cognitive processes in writing*. Hillsdale, NJ: Erlbaum.

Frase, L. T. (1970). Influence of sentence order and amount of higher level text processing upon reproductive and productive memory. *American Educational Research Journal, 7*(3), 307–319.

Frase, L. T. (1972). Maintenance and control in the acquisition of knowledge from written materials. In J. B. Carroll and R. O. Freedle (Eds.), *Language comprehension and the acquisition of knowledge.* New York: Wiley.

Freedman, S. W., Greenleaf, W. C., Sperling, M., and Parker, L. (1985). *The role of response in the acquisition of written knowledge.* Final report to the National Institute of Education. Berkeley, CA: School of Education, University of California at Berkeley.

Fulwiler, T., and Young, A. (Eds.). (1982). *Language connections: Writing and reading across the curriculum.* Urbana, IL: National Council of Teachers of English.

Gere, A. R. (Ed.). (1985). *Roots in the sawdust: Writing to learn across the disciplines.* Urbana, IL: National Council of Teachers of English.

Glover, J. A., Plake, B. S., Roberts, B., Zimmer, J. W., and Palmere, M. (1981). Distinctiveness of encoding: The effects of paraphrasing and drawing inferences on memory from prose. *Journal of Educational Psychology, 73,* 736–744.

Griffin, P., and Cole, M. (1984, March). Current activity for the future: The zo-ped. In B. Rogoff and J. V. Wertsch (Eds.), *Children's learning in the "zone of proximal development"* (pp. 45–64). New Directions for Child Development, No. 23. San Francisco: Jossey-Bass.

Hamilton, R. J. (1985). A framework for the evaluation of the effectiveness of adjunct questions and objectives. *Review of Educational Research, 55*(1), 47–85.

Hunt, K. W. (1965). *Grammatical structures written at three grade levels.* NCTE Research Report No. 3. Urbana, IL: National Council of Teachers of English.

Langer, J. A. (1980). Relation between levels of prior knowledge and the organization of recall. In M. Kamil and A. Moe (Eds.), *Perspectives on reading research and instruction* (pp. 28–33). Washington, DC: National Reading Conference.

Langer, J. A. (1981). From theory to practice: A pre-reading plan. *Journal of Reading, 25,* 152–156.

Langer, J. A. (1982). Facilitating text processing: The elaboration of prior knowledge. In J. A. Langer and M. T. Smith-Burke (Eds.), *Reader meets author: Bridging the gap.* Newark, DE: International Reading Association.

Langer, J. A. (1984a). Literacy instruction in American schools: Problems and perspectives. *American Journal of Education, 93,* 107–132.

Langer, J. A. (1984b). The effects of available information on responses to school writing tasks. *Research in the Teaching of English, 18,* 27–44.

Langer, J. A. (1984c). Examining background knowledge and text comprehension. *Reading Research Quarterly, 19*(4), 468–481.

Langer, J. A. (1986a). Learning through writing: Study skills in the content areas. *Journal of Reading, 29*(4), 400–406.

Langer, J. A. (1986b). *Children reading and writing: Structures and strategies.* Norwood, NJ: Ablex.

Langer, J. A. (1986c). Reading, writing, and understanding: An analysis of the construction of meaning. *Written Communication, 3*(2), 219–267.

Langer, J. A., and Applebee, A. N. (1984). Language, learning, and interaction: A framework for improving the teaching of writing. In A. N. Applebee, J. A. Langer, et al., *Contexts for learning to write: Studies of secondary school instruction.* Norwood, NJ: Ablex.

Langer, J. A., and Applebee, A. N. (1986). Reading and writing instruction: Toward a theory of teaching and learning. In E. Rothkopf (Ed.), *Review of Research in Education, Vol. 12.* Washington, D.C.: American Educational Research Association.

Langer, J. A., and Nicholich, M. (1981). Prior knowledge and its relationship to comprehension. *Journal of Reading Behavior, 13*, 373–379.

Maimon, E. P. (1981). *Writing in the arts and sciences.* Cambridge, MA: Winthrop.

Marland, M. (1977). *Language across the curriculum.* London: Heinemann.

Martin, N. (Ed.). (1984). *Writing across the curriculum.* Upper Montclair, NJ: Boynton/Cook. (Originally published by the University of London Institute of Education, 1973–1975.)

Martin, N., D'Arcy, P., Newton, B., and Parker, R. (1976). *Writing and learning across the curriculum, 11–16.* London: Ward Lock Educational.

Meyer, B. F. (1975). *The organization of prose and its effects on memory.* Amsterdam: North Holland.

Meyer, B. F. (1981). *Prose analysis: Procedures, purposes, and problems.* Department of Educational Psychology, College of Education, Arizona State University.

Michael, D. N., and Maccoby, N. (1961). Factors influencing the effects of student participation on verbal learning from films. In A. A. Lumsdaine (Ed.), *Student response in programmed instruction.* Washington, DC: National Academy of Sciences.

National Assessment of Educational Progress. (1978). *Reading change, 1970–1975: Summary volume* (Report No. 06-R-21). Denver: Educational Commission of the States.

National Assessment of Educational Progress. (1981). *Reading, thinking, and writing: Results from the 1979–80 national assessment of reading and literature* (Report No. 11-L-01). Denver: Educational Commission of the States.

National Commission on Excellence. (1983). *A nation at risk: The imperative for educational reform.* Washington, DC: U.S. Government Printing Office.

Newell, G. (1984). Learning from writing in two content areas: A case study/protocol analysis of writing to learn. *Research in the Teaching of English, 18*(3), 265–287.

Newkirk, T., and Atwell, N. (Eds.). (1982). *Understanding writing: Ways of observing, learning, and teaching.* Chelmsford, MA: Northeast Regional Exchange.

Palinscar, A. S., and Brown, A. L. (1984). Reciprocal teaching of comprehension-fostering and comprehension-monitoring activities. *Cognition and Instruction, 1*, 117–175.

Reder, L. M. (1980). The role of elaboration in the comprehension and retention of prose: A critical review. *Review of Educational Research, 50*(1), 5–53.

Resnick, D. P., and Resnick, L. B. (1977). The nature of literacy: An historical exploration. *Harvard Educational Review, 47*(3), 370–385.

Rothkopf, E. Z. (1966). Learning from written instructive materials: An exploration of the control of inspection behavior by test-like events. *American Educational Research Journal, 3,* 241–249.

Rothkopf, E. Z. (1972). Variable adjunct question schedules, interpersonal interaction, and incidental learning from written material. *Journal of Educational Psychology, 63,* 87–92.

Scardamalia, M. (1977). Information processing capacity and the problem of horizontal decalage: A demonstration using combinatorial reasoning tasks. *Child Development, 48,* 28–37.

Scardamalia, M., and Bereiter, C. (1985). Development of dialectical processes in composition. In D. Olson, N. Torrance, and A. Hildyard (Eds.), *Literacy, language, and learning.* New York: Cambridge University Press.

Schallert, D. L. (1976). Improving memory for prose: The relationship between depth of processing and context. *Journal of Verbal Learning and Verbal Behavior, 15,* 621–32.

Schultz, C. B., and Di Vesta, F. J. (1972). Effects of passage organization and note taking on the selection of clustering strategies and on recall of textual materials. *Journal of Educational Psychology, 63,* 244–252.

Schwartz, R. M. (1980). Levels of processing: The strategic demands of reading comprehension. *Reading Research Quarterly, 15*(4), 433–450.

Vygotsky, L. S. (1962). *Thought and language.* Cambridge, MA: Harvard University Press.

Vygotsky, L. S. (1978). *Mind in society: The development of higher psychological processes.* Cambridge, MA: Harvard University Press.

Vygotsky, L. S. (1981). The genesis of higher mental functions. In J. Wertsch (Ed.), *The concept of activity in Soviet psychology.* New York: Sharpe.

Warriner, J. E. (1951). *Handbook of English grammar and composition.* New York: Harcourt Brace Jovanovich.

Watts, G. H., and Anderson, R. C. (1971). Effects of three types of inserted questions on learning from prose. *Journal of Educational Psychology, 62,* 387–394.

Wertsch, J. V. (1979). From social interaction to higher psychological processes. A clarification and application of Vygotsky's theory. *Human Development, 22,* 1–22.

Wertsch, J. V., McNamee, G. W., McLane, J. B., and Budwig, N. A. (1980). The adult-child dyad as a problem-solving system. *Child Development, 51,* 1215–1221.

Wood, D., Bruner, J. S., and Ross, G. (1976). The role of tutoring in problem solving. *Journal of Child Psychology and Psychiatry, 17,* 89–100.

Young, A., and Fulwiler, T. (Eds.). (1986). *Writing across the disciplines: Research into practice.* Upper Montclair, NJ: Boynton/Cook.

Appendix 1
Analysis of Meaning Construction: Coding Manual[1]

Each think-aloud is segmented into distinguishable communication units. Each unit is a separately identifiable remark that expresses an idea about a thought or behavior. Because of the frequent pauses typical of the self-report activity, the researcher needs to exercise judgment in determining the boundaries of each particular remark; however, it is typically to be associated with the T-unit.

Each communication unit is categorized twice to permit analyses of (1) the reasoning operations and (2) the text unit. A communication unit is assigned (by identifying numbers) to each category on the basis of the decisions outlined below.

Reasoning Operations in Reading and Writing

The first decision is related to whether the particular comment is about reading or writing. For writing, the first digit is a 1, and for reading it is a 2. The second decision assigns the comment as to the particular reasoning operation:

.1 (Q) Questions — uncertainties and incomplete ideas that the reader or writer has at any point in the text; related to the genre, content, or text (no specified guess or expectation; moving in no specific direction).
Writing: "What will I write about?" "I don't know what I'm going to do." "Now I'm kind of wondering about where did it come from." "Let's see, what are some other things they have." (coded 1.1)
Reading: "I can't tell what it means." ". . . And I got sort of confused around there." "I was wondering how the prairie dogs saved the land." (coded 2.1)

.2 (H) Hypotheses (present) — plans, choices, or suppositions that the writer makes at the point of utterance, including choice of words or predictions that the reader makes concerning what the genre is about, what the function of a particular piece of text is, or the answer to a question, on the basis of that specific part of the text.
Writing: "When Jill was, let's say seven." "Maybe it goes into a knot." "If I should describe it or say it had a bad reputation." "I'm just going to say 'toffee'." (coded 1.2)
Reading: "They're probably big and stuff." "So maybe it's about a new kid coming to a new school." "I just found out that this could be an essay." (coded 2.2)

---

1. These coding instructions, taken from Langer (1986b), include two of the seven dimensions in the full system of analysis. Interrater agreement in the categorization of single protocol comments averaged .84; interrater reliabilities for total protocol scores, as oppposed to the categorization of individual protocol comments, averaged .97.

.3 (H) Hypotheses (future) — plans that the writer makes about what will be "said" in succeeding parts of the text, including choice of words, or predictions that the reader makes about what will be "said" in succeeding parts of the text.

Writing: "I'm going to write about something exciting happening." "I think it will be a tall man." (coded 1.3)

Reading: "It'll probably tell what they're doing and stuff." "Maybe later on, the boys will realize she's ok." (coded 2.3)

.4 (H) Hypotheses (past) — plans that the writer makes about what might now be "said" in preceding parts of the text, including word choice or hunches that the reader has about past meanings.

Writing: "Maybe I should change Western to both kinds of saddles." "I might [now] describe the person in the shuttle or something." (coded 1.4)

Reading: "Maybe it meant like rain and stuff." (coded 2.4)

.5 (A) Assumptions — meanings that the writer assumes need no further explanation or elaboration, or meanings that the reader takes for granted without textual evidence.

Writing: "That sort of tells it all." "In a little short story, it's not enough really." (coded 1.5)

Reading: "There's nothing to think about." "Right there I knew it was a weapon." (coded 2.5)

.6 (S) Schemata — the ideas being developed or explained on the basis of the genre, content, or text.

Writing: "The hammerhead shark is the largest in the world." "She thought she had tied her shoe." "They have populations of really small cities." (coded 1.6)

Reading: "There are hardly any left." "This tells me the mole has weird ears." "A different school might be different from her school." (coded 2.6)

.7 (SP) Schemata personalized — personal experiences drawn upon by the writer or reader.

Writing: "Those were the kind I liked." "I practice a lot everyday." "Sports are my main interest." "I don't remember when I went to nursery school." (coded 1.7)

Reading: "I've never been sent to bed without dinner." "I can see this kid going to my teacher and saying hi." (coded 2.7)

.8 (SE) Schemata (or hypotheses) evaluated — evaluations and judgments being made about what is written or read.

Writing: "That's not right." "That sounds dumb." "They are different ideas." "Oh, I was wrong. . . ." (coded 1.8)

Reading: "That's funny." "That's not so." "It's pretty good." (coded 2.8)

.9 (SL) Schematic links — concept links that the writer or reader makes.

Writing: "The flying and jumping could go together to make a great big flying leap." (coded 1.9)

Reading: "They talked tough and acted tough and fought with him." (coded 2.9)

.10 (MC) Metacomments: content — comments about the writer's or reader's use or nonuse of particular content information.

Writing: "I decided not to use it." "No, I won't do that." "I might put these things in different words." (coded 1.10)

Reading: "I kept on reading [the ideas]." "That's the only thing I can think of." (coded 2.10)

.11 (MC) Metacomments: text — comments about the writer's or reader's use or nonuse of particular surface features of the text itself.

Writing: "Some of these sentences are short and choppy and some are long." "I might put these in different order." "I put we instead of when." "Put a comma there." (coded 1.11)

Reading: "The quotes mean she's talking." (coded 2.11)

.12 (E) Evidence — the information that the writer presents, the explanations that the writer provides, or the evidence that the writer develops to answer a question, carry out a hypothesis, or fill in the schemata; or information that the reader gathers or explanations the reader provides to answer a question or to confirm or disconfirm a hypothesis. Includes all direct or implied statements of causality.

Writing: ". . .Because you can get hurt on the right side." "Cause its expensive." "That's how I know how to spell penny loafers." (coded 1.12)

Reading: "You can tell he's the leader." "He's trying to make a fight." "Cause it says it was made by a small furry animal called a mole." (coded 2.12)

.13 (V) Validations — information, implied or direct, that the plan was fulfilled or a decision made.

Writing: "That's what it was." "Well, that's what they're like." "So he had a fight." "I decided not to." "All right, that's about it." (coded 1.13)

Reading: "So, the prairie dog was a hero." "I've seen it before." "OK, that tells me the same thing." "So the title doesn't fit really." (coded 2.13)

Text Unit

1. (L) Local — attention is focused on localized points within the text.
2. (G) Global — attention is focused on the overall message of the entire piece.

Appendix 2
The Reading Passages:
Synopses, Characteristics,
and Tree Diagrams

Economic Expansion

This passage traces industrial growth in the United States from the Civil War until the early 1900s, by which point the United States had emerged as the leading industrial nation. Several factors of growth are discussed, including natural resources, the growth of railroads, a growing labor force, available capital, new technology, and favorable government attitudes. The passage is loosely organized, with many specific but undeveloped examples to support its main points. (Source: G. M. Linden, E. A. Wassenich, D. C. Brink, and W. J. Jones, Jr. [1979]. *History of our American republic* [pp. 431–432]. River Forest, IL: Laidlaw.)

Postwar Russia

This passage traces the political and economic history of the Soviet Union from the end of World War II through the beginning of Krushchev's rule. Topics include Stalin's five-year-plans to meet the problems of postwar reconstruction; the imposition of Communist rule in Eastern Europe; Tito's independence in Yugoslavia; and Krushchev's attempts to raise the standard of living as well as to develop heavy industry and military weaponry. (Source: T. W. Wallbank and A. Schrier. [1974]. *Living world history* [3rd ed.] [pp. 687-689]. Glenview, IL: Scott Foresman.)

The Great Depression

After describing the prosperity of the 1920s, this passage moves to the stock market crash in 1929 and the spread of the depression in the years that followed. Several conflicting explanations of the Great Depression are mentioned, with no attempt to resolve the disagreement. The passage ends with a chronology of Hoover's responses during the early years of depression, making the point that the President had accepted for the first time the idea that the federal government must assume some responsibility when the economy suffers. (Source: L. P. Todd and M. Curti. [1982]. *Rise of the American nation*, Liberty Edition, [pp. 555–558]. New York: Harcourt Brace Jovanovich.)

Twentieth Century Science

This passage details the variety of effects that modern science has had on contemporary life. Topics include new comforts and conveniences, the development of assembly-line production, medical advances, industrialization, and the extent to which scientists and scientific advances have become front-page news. The passage is structured as a variety of elaborations on the central theme of scientific progress, with little connection among the sections. (Source: C. J. H. Hayes and M. Faissler. [1965]. *Modern times: The French revolution to the present* [pp. 507–510]. London: Macmillan.)

Table 21

Characteristics of the Reading Passages

Short Title	Number of Words	Textbook Level	Readability Level[a]
Economic expansion	766	Grade 11	Grade 10
Postwar Russia	1,123	Grade 9	Grade 12
Great depression	1,721	Grade 11	College
Twentieth century science	837	Grade 11	Grade 12

[a] Based on Fry formula.

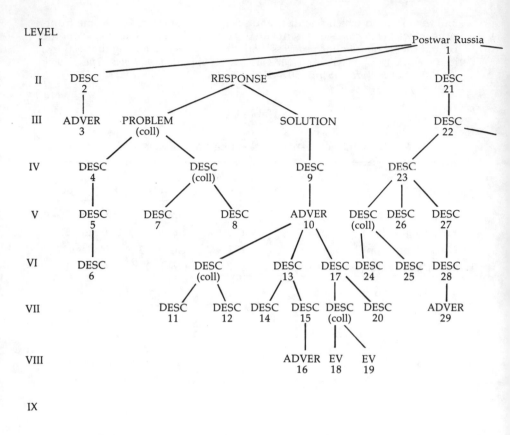

Tree diagram 1. Key content nodes in reading passage on postwar Russia. See Fig. 1, p. 166 for key content and key to abbreviations.

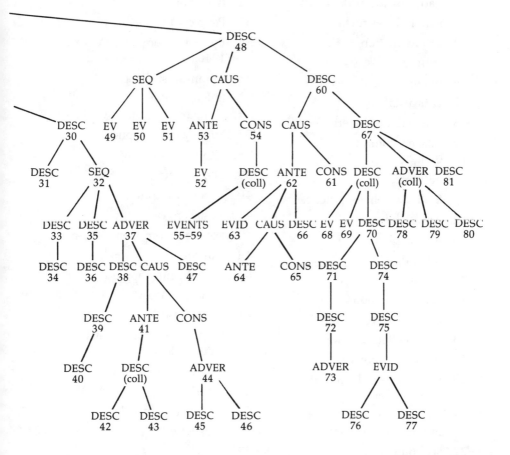

1. Postwar Russia
2. had army, territory
3. suffered destruction
4. reconstruction
5. suffered most
6. millions killed, destroyed
7. critical tasks
8. consolidate Eastern Europe
9. relaxed control
10. Stalin restored CCP authority
11. Stalinist beliefs, practices
12. censorship
13. 5-year plans
14. rebuild, expand
15. industrial doubled
16. consumer goods scarce
17. controlled agriculture
18. mass collectivization
19. peasants supervised
20. incentive production 10% higher
21. communist revolutions in Eastern Europe
22. six countries
23. common characteristics
24. peasants
25. poor
26. upper classes no reform
27. discredited ruling groups
28. peasant parties
29. leaders intellectuals
30. Red Army

31. Soviet-style revolution
32. two stages
33. People's Democracy
34. Bulgaria, Romania, Poland 1946
35. Communist dictator
36. Bulgaria, Romania, Poland, Hungary, Czechoslovakia 1953
37. Yugoslavia exception
38. Tito without troops
39. Tito, resistance
40. Yugoslavs united
41. Stalin angry
42. expelled from Cominform
43. withdrew aid
44. Tito did not topple
45. turned to West
46. loosened rule
47. Yugoslavian communist independence
48. Stalin's death changes
49. Stalin
50. leadership struggle
51. Krushchev
52. speech
53. denounced Stalin
54. deStalinization
55. camps
56. police
57. writers
58. exchanges
59. tourists
60. Krushchev changes

Figure 1. Key content (by node number) and key to abbreviations for postwar Russia tree diagram.

61. shortages
62. rural migration
63. in cities
64. demanded production
65. demanded incentive
66. middle class
67. desires
68. TV, clothes
69. housing
70. total production
71. industry up, agriculture lagged
72. tried schemes
73. barely kept pace
74. emphasized military, industrial, space
75. impressive results
76. A-bomb, H-bomb
77. satellite, spaceman, landing
78. clothes
79. housing
80. highways
81. economy not all consumer

DESC = Description
ADVER = Adversative
SEQ   = Sequence
CAUS = Causal
coll = collection
EV   = Event
ANTE = Antecedent
CONS = Consequence

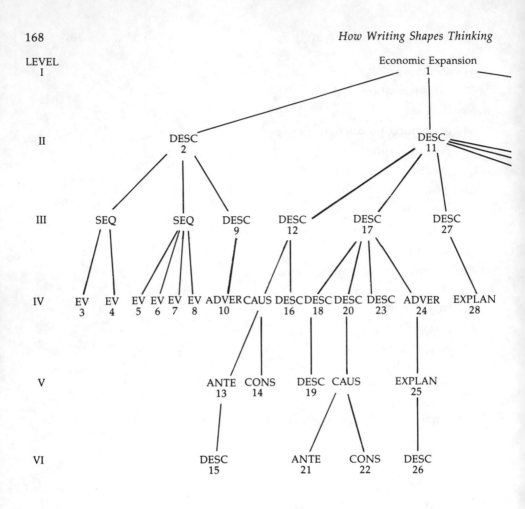

Tree diagram 2. Key content nodes in reading passage on economic expansion. See Fig. 2, p. 170 for key content and key to abbreviations.

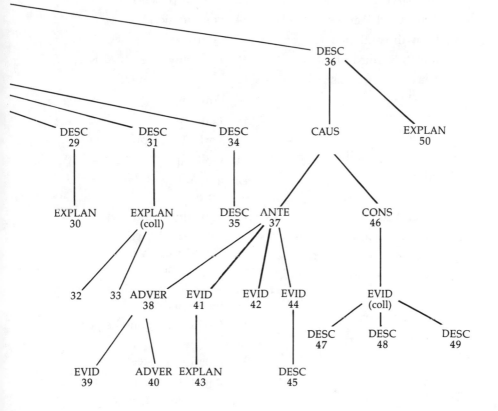

1. Economic Expansion
2. Industrial growth
3. After Civil War
4. Growth continued
5. fourth to third place
6. one-third of industrial production
7. France and Great Britain
8. 24 billion
9. Technology and immigration
10. other
11. Factors of growth
12. Several reasons
13. Started during Civil War
14. To meet demands
15. factories in north
16. 79% increase
17. Natural resources
18. coal
19. Over 30%
20. oil
21. Production grew
22. By 1914
23. other raw materials
24. little use
25. Thus, railroads
26. 260,000 miles
27. Labor helped
28. workers available
29. availability of money
30. from profits
31. improved technology

32. technology
33. federal policies
34. combination
35. GNP
36. Economy in early '20s
37. growth continued
38. Although
39. Panic of 1907
40. Early 1900s prosperous
41. GNP up 500% 1900–1920
42. amount manufactured up 32%
43. agriculture and service occupations
44. 100% growth in employment
45. 40 million full-time by 1920
46. Good conditions helped industry
47. meat, iron, steel
48. paper, chemicals, petroleum
49. automobile 4 billion
50. Thus, most industries

DESC   = Description
ADVER   = Adversative
SEQ   = Sequence
CAUS   = Causal
coll   = collection
EV   = Event
ANTE   = Antecedent
CONS   = Consequence
EXPLAN = Explanation

Figure 2. Key content (by node number) and key to abbreviations for economic expansion tree diagram.

Authors

Judith A. Langer is a professor of education at the State University of New York at Albany. An educational psychologist, she is interested in issues of language and thought. Her research focuses on literacy — on how people become skilled readers and writers, on how they use reading and writing to learn, and on what this means for instruction. In collaboration with the National Assessment of Educational Progress, Professor Langer has analyzed trends and has written the last seven monographs on reading and writing. These monographs discuss achievement in light of home, instructional, and policy variables and recommend new directions for reading and writing education. She has authored and edited several books on literacy and learning and has also published in a wide range of educational journals and collections. Professor Langer is coeditor of *Research in the Teaching of English.*

Arthur N. Applebee is a professor in the School of Education, State University of New York at Albany. He specializes in studies of language use and language learning, particularly as these occur in school settings. Some of Professor Applebee's major works include a developmental study of children's storytelling and story-comprehension skills, a national study of the teaching of writing in the major secondary school subject areas, and a comprehensive history of the teaching of literature in American secondary schools. Professor Applebee is coauthor of a series of reports on reading and writing achievement from the national Assessment of Educational Progress. He has experience in program evaluation, high school teaching (English and drama), and clinical assessment and treatment of children with severe reading problems. Professor Applebee is coeditor of *Research in the Teaching of English* and is past president of the National Conference on Research in English.